The Nature of Expertise
in Professional Acting:
A Cognitive View

Expertise: Research and Applications

Robert R. Hoffman, K. Anders Ericsson, Gary Klein, Dean K. Simonton,
Robert J. Sternberg, and Christopher D. Wickens, **Series Editors**

Hoc/Caccibue/Hollnagel (1995) *Expertise and Technology: Issues in Cognition and Human–Computer Interaction*

Zsambok/Klein (1997) *Naturalistic Decision Making*

Noice/Noice (1997) *The Nature of Expertise in Professional Acting: A Cognitive View*

The Nature of Expertise in Professional Acting: A Cognitive View

Tony Noice
Indiana State University
Helga Noice
Augustana College

LAWRENCE ERLBAUM ASSOCIATES, PUBLISHERS
1997   Mahwah, New Jersey   London

Copyright © 1997 by Lawrence Erlbaum Associates, Inc.
All rights reserved. No part of this book may be reproduced in
any form, by photostat, microform, retrieval system, or any other
means, without the prior written permission of the publisher.

Lawrence Erlbaum Associates, Inc., Publishers
10 Industrial Avenue
Mahwah, New Jersey 07430

Library of Congress Cataloging-in-Publication-Data

    Noice, Tony.
The nature of expertise in professional acting: a cognitive view/ Tony
Noice, Helga Noice
      p. cm.
    Includes bibliographical references and index.
    ISBN 0-8058-2169-4 (cloth: alk. paper). – ISBN 0-8058-2170-
8 (pbk.: alk. paper)
    1. Actors—Psychology. 2. Acting. I. Noice, Helga
    PN2058.N65 1997
    792' .028' 019—dc21   97-12571
                                                    CIP

Books published by Lawrence Erlbaum Associates are printed on
acid-free paper, and their bindings are chosen for strength and durability.

Printed in the United States of America
10 9 8 7 6 5 4 3 2 1

To actors and psychologists everywhere. Taking different paths, they work toward the same goal: discovering the truth of human behavior.

Contents

	Series Editor's Preface	ix
	Introduction	xi
1	Training for the Profession	1
2	Psychological Research Into Actors' Mental Processes	10
3	Experimental Investigation of Actors' Learning Strategies	19
4	Cued Recall Task	36
5	The Summarization Task and Posttest Statements of Strategy	48
6	A Professional Actor Prepares a Role: A Think-Aloud Protocol	55
7	More Think-Aloud Protocols	71
8	A Mnemonist's Approach to Script Learning	77
9	The Benefits of Script Segmentation	87
10	Continuing the Quest	99
11	A General Model of Acting Cognition	114
12	Other Investigations of Actors and Acting	118

Appendix A: Scene From *The Second Man* by S. N. Behrman … 123

Appendix B: Protocol of T. D. … 129

Appendix C: Sample Page of an Annotated Script … 135

References … 137

Author Index … 147

Subject Index … 151

Series Editor's Preface

This volume is the third to appear in the Expertise Series, but it is the first authored volume. We hope that many more will follow. This volume is also noteworthy because it is the first to focus on one particular domain, in this case, that of professional acting. One might note in passing that this domain is not one of those that is familiar to cognitive science (i.e., chess, computer programming, physics problem solving, and the like). It is for the better that the field of expertise studies looks at "new" domains, for it is only through the widest possible sampling that we may grasp confident and general facts.

The authors of this volume are to be commended for combining their own acting and teaching experience with their skills as experimental psychologists in a rich series of experimental investigations. Hence, this volume may serve as guidance for those who may follow in the desire to study some particular domain in depth. The study of expertise affords opportunities for experimental psychologists to combine their personal interests with their work as scientists. This intrinsic motivation or self-fulfilling aspect of the study of expertise is one thing that offsets the formidable theoretical and methodological challenges of exploring new territory.

INTRODUCTION

For nearly 25 years, expertise has been considered an important testing ground for theories of cognition. Cognitive scientists have examined experts as diverse as chess masters (Chase & Simon, 1973), waiters (Ericsson & Polson, 1988), field-hockey players (Starkes & Deakin, 1985), and computer programmers (Soloway, Adelson, & Ehrlich, 1988). Recently, increased attention has been given to the arts, including dance (Solso & Dallop, 1995), music appreciation and performance (Ericsson, Lehmann, & Taylor, 1993; Sloboda, 1991), and literary analysis (Graves & Frederiksen, 1991; Scardamalia & Bereiter, 1991). It is therefore somewhat surprising that, except for the authors' program of research dating from the late 1980s, virtually no studies on the cognitive processes of professional actors can be found in the literature. Yet these experts not only routinely memorize hours worth of verbal material in a very short time, but they retrieve it verbatim along with the accompanying gestures, movements, thoughts, and emotions of the characters. The mental processes involved in this task constitute the subject of our recent research and are described in detail in this book.

THEORIES OF EXPERTISE

In 1984 Glaser (along with Chi and Lesgold), proposed a theory of expertise based largely on the investigation of problem solving in physics and radiology (Chi, Feltovich, & Glaser, 1981; Chi, Glaser, & Rees, 1982; Lesgold, Feltovich, Glaser, & Wang, 1981). In the view of Glaser and his associates, an expert's mental representation of a problem is qualitatively different from that of a novice: The latter represents a problem in terms of the literal cues available in the problem description; the former represents the same problem based on higher-order principles derived from an interaction between the problem description and a large, well-organized knowledge base. This proclivity of experts to represent problems on deeper or more principled levels has also been reported in solving algebra-word problems (Hinsley, Hayes, & Simon, 1977), in reading circuit diagrams (Egan & Schwartz, 1979), in recalling computer programming language (McKeithen, Reitman, Reuter, & Hirtle, 1981), and even in exploring ill-defined problem areas (Voss & Post, 1988).

This rapidly increasing body of research tended to center on expert–novice differences and indicated that experts not only possess vastly more domain specific, conceptual, and procedural knowledge, but that they are able to access it far more efficiently. Drawing on this burgeoning corpus of inquiry, Glaser (1987) isolated 10 points that he felt characterized expertise in a wide variety of domains. These points included continuous development of competence (Chi, Glaser, & Farr, 1988); specificity of expertise (Carey, 1985); the ability to make analogies between one's own domain and those of others (Gentner & Gentner, 1983); the ability to develop self-regulatory processes (Brown, Collins, & Harris, 1978; Gitomer & Glaser, 1987); the ability to perceive large meaningful patterns (Lesgold, 1984; Chi et al., 1982); and the goal-oriented nature of experts' knowledge (Voss, Greene, Post, & Penner, 1983). However, only the two latter points appear to have direct relevance to our own findings on the process of professional acting. (As is shown in chap. 9, actors frequently segment a to-be-learned script according to the plans of the characters, resulting in large, goal-directed chunks of dialogue.)

Thus, expert actors appear to share few of the essential attributes of experts in other fields. More importantly, the domains to which Glaser referred were characterized by the demand for extensive, highly specific knowledge, whereas the principles by which actors render roles are relatively few and impossible to specify. Indeed, our investigations with actors show that they depend largely on their moment-to-moment (i.e., spontaneous) responses during performance. Dreyfus and Dreyfus (1986) argued that this type of spontaneous response constitutes a major stumbling block for any eventual theory of expertise:

> A boxer seems to recognize the moment to begin an attack, not by combining by rule various facts about his body's position and that of his opponent, but when the whole visual scene in front of him and sensations within him trigger the memory of earlier similar situations in which an attack was successful. We call the intuitive ability to use patterns without decomposing them into component features "holistic similarity recognition." (p. 28)

Furthermore, Dreyfus and Dreyfus (1986), in discussing computer simulation of expertise, expressed doubt that machines will ever be capable of human-like thinking. For instance, they questioned whether a computer would eventually be able to recognize emotion in a face because emotion cannot be broken down into elementary symbols.

However, some researchers are currently trying to construct virtual reality programs that will give users at least the illusion of emotion. One such enterprise, called "The Oz Project," is being developed by Joseph Bates and his colleagues at Carnegie Mellon (e.g., Kelso, Weyhrauch, & Bates, 1993). This artificial intelligence (AI) system is designed to create within the viewer a necessary suspension of disbelief that Bates accomplishes by using characters who appear to be eccentric, lovable, and capable of displaying emotions. The state of this research and the attendant problems are taken up in chapter 12.

In spite of the inherent difficulties of examining the nature of expertise in the arts, an extensive research program has been carried out by Anders

Ericsson and his collaborators (e.g., Ericsson & Charness, 1994; Ericsson, Krampe, & Tesch-Roemer, 1993; Ericsson & Lehmann, 1996). In addition to investigating skill acquisition in specific disciplines, these authors distilled several principles that these disciplines have in common, for the purpose of deriving a general theory of expertise. Their findings led them to believe that innate talent is not the critical determinant of eventual expertise and that, if hereditary influences do exist, the locus of these influences is apt to lie within motivational factors (Ericsson, Krampe et al., 1993). Furthermore, Ericsson and his colleagues posit that expertise is generally a result of extended training that "alters the cognitive and physiological processes of experts to a greater degree than is commonly believed possible" (Ericsson & Charness, 1994, p. 726).

Skepticism of this position has been expressed by Sternberg (1996), who said, "The practice view cannot begin to account for the success of extraordinary achievers in the creative domains, and as far as I can tell, its exponents have not made a serious effort to do so" (p. 351). Nevertheless, Ericsson and his associates appear to hold to their belief that properly directed, deliberate practice is the true determinant of expert performance.

Of course, the nature of deliberate practice varies among domains. In some, the practice is largely mental (e.g., chess); in others, it is largely physical (e.g., running); whereas in still others, it is both mental and physical (e.g., violin playing). However, regardless of the type of practice, its disciplined application is thought to be the critical element. For example, it has been shown that chess expertise varies systematically with the number of books read by players in which games of the masters have been recreated (Charness, Krampe, & Mayr, 1996).

THE NATURE OF ACTING EXPERTISE

However, the application of these notions to actors is problematical. Unlike the situation with violinists, ballet dancers, or distance runners, practice in acting does not seem to make perfect. A professor in a large state university once said that even after 4 years of university training, not more than 1 in 100 students had the basic skill to successfully compete in open auditions for small supporting roles in professional theater (B. Wickes, personal communication, September 4, 1990). Other educators have found the failure–success ratio to be even higher. (These pessimistic predictions concern only acting *skill*. When one includes such important factors as appearance, personality, and self-marketing ability, the percentage of college-trained actors who actually make a full time living in theater is far lower.) According to Actors Equity Association (AEA), there are approximately 1,000 members (out of over 30,000) who earn above $25,000 a year exclusively from stage work ("Equity News," 1994). And there are far more university-trained actors who have yet to get their first professional job, enabling them to join the union. These figures indicate that fewer than 1% of trained actors make a full time living in live theater. Yet producers, directors, and writers consistently report that finding suitable actors capable of meeting the requirements of demanding roles is their biggest problem. Neil Simon said that it takes 3 to 6 months to properly cast a play with only a half dozen characters, and a playwright of his eminence has the choice of the most skilled stage actors in America (Simon, 1991). Certainly, a great many of those who lack the ability to compete successfully are not unmotivated. Typically, after majoring in theater in college, these actors work as waiters, taxi drivers, and office temps to pay for a never-ending regime of acting workshops, voice lessons, dance classes, and the like, without ever acquiring a professional level of competency.

Thus, it appears that many of the factors isolated in expertise research do not result in the sufficiently high degree of skill necessary to compete in professional theater. This is perhaps because even highly motivated effort (in terms of repetitive practice) plays a small role. Indeed, most acting classes involve one of two types of training, neither of which entails repetitive practice. The first type consists of exercises that are designed to free the actor's emotions and disinhibit expressiveness. These range from relatively benign *theater games* to controversial exercises such as *the death bed* in which the actor visualizes a loved one to whose dead body the actor pours out his or her most private feelings in front of the class (Mekler, 1987).

The other type of acting training is referred to as *scene study* and consists of duplicating the performance experience. The actors rehearse a scene on their own and present it to the class for feedback from the director. More often than not, the criticism centers around notions such as the scene appearing predictable or lacking the juices of real life.

In a way, the heart of skillful acting technique is the opposite of the type of skill acquired when a musician practices scales or a tennis player works on a serve. The actor is always told not to bring in what was rehearsed yesterday, but to do the scene now—for the first time. The only repetitive practice involved in acting training entails the acquisition of collateral skills, such as strengthening and cultivating the speaking voice by means of vocal exercises, or keeping the physical instrument (the actor's body) in peak condition through dance training, fencing, acrobatics, and so on. This is not to say that actors do not improve by virtue of continued effort. However, the improvement does not come as a result of deliberate practice but of repeated performance. In effect, every performance is a practice session in the creation of spontaneity.

The benefit of experience over practice has been shown in other fields. Ericsson, Lehmann et al. (1993) studied sight reading ability among musicians and concluded that deliberate practice, while increasing this proficiency somewhat, was inferior to working experience (as an accompanist) for enhancement of that particular ability. This implies a separate, domain-specific benefit of experience. However, skill in accompanying is primarily of value to a musician who is content to be a supporting artist and not a solo performer. The opposite situation appears to be true in acting. Deliberate practice increases the actor's technical proficiency in terms of vocal and bodily skills but, in the opinion of most experts, on-stage performing experience is indispensable for acquiring skill in the acting process itself. This points to a contrast between acting and other forms of performing arts. In music, dance, etc. (as well as in sports) deliberate practice is the most significant element in gaining proficiency in the most prized aspect of the profession: outstanding performance. But in acting, deliberate practice only enhances collateral attributes.

Nevertheless, Ericsson's *10-year rule*, the notion that 10 or more years of intense preparation are necessary for the attainment of expertise (Ericsson & Lehman, 1996), has often been assumed to also apply to acting. For instance, one book (based on the NYU acting class of director/playwright David Mamet, and actor Bill Macy) discussed the principles of spontaneous acting and stated, "As simple as they are, we believe it will take you ten or fifteen years to master them" (Bruder, Cohn, Olnek, Pollack, Previto, & Zigler, 1986, p. 85). This is not an unusual opinion; Joanne Woodward quoted her acting teacher, Sanford Meisner, as saying that proficiency took 20 years to acquire (Pollack, 1984).

MUSICAL EXPERTISE

Some efforts have been made to address the nature of skill acquisition in domains where progress is not made primarily by repetitive practice. For example, Sloboda (1991) offered five conditions that he felt were crucial to the molding of an expert musical performer:

1. Existence in a musical culture of forms that have perceptible structures of certain kinds ...
2. Frequent informal exposure to examples of these forms over a lifetime.
3. Existence of a normal range of human emotional responses.
4. Opportunity to experience these emotions mediated through perceived musical structures ...
5. Opportunity to experience music in contexts free of externally imposed constraints or negative reinforcements. (p. 168)

Sloboda used the life of the legendary jazz musician Louis Armstrong to illustrate his five conditions. Many other jazz musicians must have been subject to the same nurturing circumstances, but Armstrong's reputation as a standard bearer is such that one of the cliches in the field is, "If you don't love Louis, you're nothing." Musician/critic Wynton Marsalis (1996) said that Armstrong's recorded solos were impossible to duplicate, not just because of their extraordinary demands on technique, but because no trumpet player, before or since, has ever had that control of nuance. As superb a technician as Armstrong was, there were others who were equally skilled. How then, does one account for his exceptional ability? The answer would appear to lie in the individual resources Armstrong brought to his playing, and it does not seem possible, at this time, to determine whether some part of these resources were inborn or were all simply conditioned by a confluence of fortuitous circumstances in his early life.

Therefore, we believe that Sloboda's (1991) statement, "If we can insure these conditions, then the problems associated with bringing individuals to levels of achievement we would currently regard as exceptional may turn out to be trivial" may well be true in many cases (p. 169). However, we feel that there is still some legitimate doubt about how trivial those problems would be when it comes to producing extraordinary performing talents like Louis Armstrong or Laurence Olivier.

OTHER FACTORS IN PERFORMING ARTISTS' EXPERTISE

Indeed, with artists whose work is a seamless blend of technique and emotion, properly directed practice seems to only account for the technique part, and a complete theory of emotion is still not on the horizon. Moreover, in acting, the contribution of technique is of somewhat less importance than in music, dance, or sports, and while there has been some research involving actors' emotions, the factors underlying their use in performance were not examined. (For example, Ekman, Levenson, & Friesen, 1983, investigated the universality of facial expressions connoting various emotions by having actors reproduce these expressions, and Futterman, Kemeny, Shapiro, Polonsky, & Fahey, 1992 found changes in blood chemistry when actors imaginatively relived highly emotional experiences.)

Furthermore, acting is not the type of skill referred to by Charness et al. (in press) as *entrepreneurial*, in which ability is acquired by intense reading of relevant literature. According to most theater practitioners, the heart of acting skill is the ability to commit oneself fully to the character's situation under the highly artificial conditions imposed by professional performance. Fine actors are fully aware they are on stage, but they *choose* to immerse themselves in the character's ongoing reality, resulting in behavior that is exciting, unpredictable, and palpably alive. Perhaps the potential to acquire this ability is not innate but is a result of parental encouragement of fantasy early in life. Indeed, some prominent acting theorists regard daydreaming as an indispensable component in the preparation of a role (Silverberg, 1994). However, in this book we do not enter the debate over whether or not inborn talent is necessary to the attainment of acting expertise and concentrate instead on our research into the specific cognitive learning strategies expert actors employ in preparing roles.

Solso and Dallop (1995) took this approach when they investigated dancers' acquisition of new patterns, and showed that dancers frequently falsely recognize a base pattern (learned in the past) as one of a new series of patterns just shown to them. Furthermore, the more features the new patterns shared with the base pattern, the more the dancers tended to falsely recognize the base pattern. The authors concluded that dancers, at least in the early stages of learning new steps, "form a prototype from a set of exemplars that is composed of frequently experienced features" (p. 10).

Chaffin (1994) studied the process by which a musician (a concert pianist) memorized a piece for her repertoire. The process consisted of breaking the score into very small units. The more difficult the fingering, the smaller the units. The first unit was practiced separately until it could be properly executed, then the second was practiced. When smoothly performed, it was added to the previous unit and the two were practiced together. The third unit was worked on separately, then added to the first two, and so on. When a section had been learned in this fashion, it was committed to memory as part of the overall structure of the piece. Finally, the pianist reported that when the entire piece had been learned, the dominant thought during performance was the emotion that the pianist wished to convey. As is seen in later chapters, this procedure is far different from that used by most professional actors during script learning.

ACTORS' LEARNING STRATEGIES

One attribute of the professional actor is the possession of a somewhat unique learning strategy that involves analysis rather than repetition, and that enables the performer to maintain spontaneous involvement in the present moment of the drama while retrieving the upcoming lines without hesitation from long-term memory. With many novice actors, the latter appears to be an either-or situation. While they initially read the script with intelligence and purpose, when they have to perform from memory during early rehearsals, it is apparent from their demeanor (i.e., hesitations, blank expressions, and looking at the floor or ceiling) that they are searching for upcoming lines. With sufficient drilling, they eventually recall the words without hesitation, but their delivery often sounds flat and mechanical. In the view of many acting teachers, these novices cannot commit themselves fully to the dramatic situation because much of their mental capacity is being used to retrieve the exact words of the script (e.g., R. Cohen, personal communication, September 29, 1995). Indeed, one hallmark of professional actors appears to be that they have consciously or unconsciously discovered an optimal way to memorize a script, one that not only allows them to efficiently retrieve the scripted dialogue, but to do so while being engrossed in the emotional experience of the moment.

In our own studies described in this book, no actor seemed to be explicitly aware of a connection between emotionally truthful performance and script-learning strategy. This is possibly due to their early training; there is little advice on role memorization given in theater courses, and what there is varies from instructor to instructor, from textbook to textbook. One of the most respected acting teachers of the century, Sanford Meisner, tells his students to learn by rote (Meisner & Longwell, 1987). This view has been strongly endorsed by playwright/director David Mamet (Bruder et al., 1986). Yet, a number of actors and acting teachers insist that they use the opposite approach, claiming that if the thinking of the character is developed with sufficient specificity, the actor will absorb the text completely without explicit line-by-line memorization (e.g., Funke & Booth, 1961). Regardless of the approach used, most professional actors appear to acquire a mental representation of the text that allows them to simultaneously retrieve the stored material and the cognitive/affective concomitants of that material. Ericsson and Lehmann (1996) pointed out that in order to study expert performance, one must identify the essence of expertise as opposed to other tasks at which the expert would probably excel. For example, superior memory for the positions of the chess pieces, although possessed by most chess masters, would not capture the essence of their expertise, but the ability to select superior chess moves for a given configuration of pieces would. Most theater practitioners and theorists agree that the essence of acting is living truthfully under imaginary circumstances. That is, if the actor is portraying a 16th-century Spanish king who is angrily denouncing his traitorous councilors, although the situation is predetermined by the memorized text, the actor's denouncement of the other actors and the accompanying anger are real at the moment of performance.

This dualism appears to be central to expertise. The text is retrieved from long-term memory, but the actor's concentration is on affecting the other actors *at the time of utterance*. In other words, the essence of acting is simply to use the memorized text to actually do *anew*, at every performance, what the character would do within the particular dramatic situation.

The way in which this dual process is handled seems to point to one important difference between novices and experts. Student actors are routinely instructed to keep all their attention on the other actor/characters within the dramatic situation. In order to follow these instructions, many students appear to convert their performances into examples of automatic and controlled processing (Schneider & Shiffrin, 1977). The memorized words are made accessible by dint of long practice. Consequently, the student can keep all of his or her attention on the on-stage situation (controlled processing) while still retrieving and speaking the exact words of the text (automatic processing). As a result of this separation, student performances can fail to be completely convincing. It seems plausible that the cognitive processes of professional actors have become altered (as Ericsson has suggested for experts in other domains) so that the retrieval of the memorized material is automatic but its production is deliberate.

Some psycholinguists (e.g., Clark & Clark, 1977) regard articulation as the final step in the multistage planning/execution process of speech production. As is seen in the subsequent chapters of this book, actors consistently analyze their characters' plans in great detail, and this effort may result in activation of the various stages of this speech production process during performance. Barsalou (1992) regarded speech production as an example of strategic processing and distinguished between automatic and executive productions. The latter involves processing in which both current contextual information and goal information in memory interact. In Barsalou's view, "The primary difference between automatic and executive productions revolves around the experience of conscious willful control" (p. 74). As shown later in chapters 3, 6, and 7, the protocols of expert actors frequently reveal this willful control of the interactions between contextual and goal information.

In our research of how actors perform memorized material with apparently complete spontaneity (e. g., Noice, 1992), we have concentrated thus far on one vital aspect of acting expertise: role acquisition. Because this research has shown a link between the way most actors process a script and their eventual, spontaneous yet verbatim performance of it, a case could be made that role acquisition is indeed the essence of acting. However, without even going that far, we still feel that the prodigious memories of expert actors are a fruitful area of investigation.

Oliver and Ericsson (1986) have shown that actors can rapidly recall lines from anywhere in the script with one- or two-word prompts, suggesting that this mental representation is not accessed serially. But what is the specific nature of an actor's mental representation that allows him or her to retrieve lengthy material verbatim while performing it spontaneously? What kinds of elaborations are generated during script learning? What organizational schemes are employed? Are there large individual differences or are certain mental processes common to almost all actors? How do actors transfer written scripts into conversation so that they relive the dialogue rather than recall it? Our program of research set out to answer these questions; this book addresses them as follows:

Chapter 1 discusses an actor's training and reviews the relevant theater literature. Chapter 2 describes the pilot study (Noice, 1992) that launched our investigations and gave rise to the experiments reported in chapters 3, 4, and 5 (Noice, 1991, 1993). Subsequent research involved collecting think-aloud protocols; the analysis of these is described in chapters 6 and 7 (Noice & Noice, 1994, 1996a). Chapter 8 is devoted to the analysis of a protocol generated by a well-known professional mnemonist and to a comparison between that protocol and those generated by actors for the same theatrical scene (Noice & Noice, 1996a). Because our research consistently showed that, before learning a script, actors divide it into segments they call *beats*, chapter 9 describes an experiment designed to investigate the benefits of this type of script division (Noice & Noice, 1993a, 1993b). In chapter 10, we describe three new experiments, one of which involved training acting students to use experts' strategies. Chapter 11 is devoted to the presentation of a professional actor's mental model, with special emphasis on the memory component. In chapter 12, we discuss some additional experiments with actors, performed by a variety of investigators, as well as some of our own in various stages of completion. A brief conclusion summarizes our findings.

ACKNOWLEDGMENTS

The authors would like to thank Robert R. Hoffman, Micki T. H. Chi, K. Anders Ericsson, and Gary A. Klein, the editors of the LEA book series, *Expertise: Research and Applications* when this volume was propsed. We are particularly grateful to Robert Hoffman, who originally suggested this book and supplied invaluable advice and recommendations on the first draft.

We also wish to acknowledge our Acquisitions Editor, Ray O'Connell, Editorial Assistant, Sara Scudder, and Production Editor, Nicole Bush, at Lawrence Erlbaum Associates, as well as the scores of professional actors who gave of their time and talents so that we might extend our scientific knowledge of the mysteries of their beautiful and unusual craft. In addition, we thank Chuck Schmidt, whose deep interest in plan theory inspired our own, and our many students who aided in the collection, preparation, analysis, and presentation of the data.

Some of the writing took place during the second author's sabbatical and she wishes to acknowledge the generosity of the Augustana Faculty Research Committee in awarding her an Augustana College/Augustana Research Foundation Sabbatical Stipend.

1

Training for the Profession

More than 100 actors participated in our 8-year program of studies (Noice, 1991, 1992, 1993; Noice & Noice, 1993a, 1993b, 1994, 1996a, 1996b). Except for some recent studies with student actors (e. g., Noice & Noice, 1997), the overwhelming majority of participants had both university training and at least 10 years of experience as full-time, card-carrying professionals. It is assumed that their current expertise is a product of their training, modified or enhanced by practice. This chapter concentrates on the former element by presenting an overview of acting theory as presented in text books and by instructors, examining areas of agreement and disagreement, particularly in the domain of script learning.

MODERN HISTORY OF ACTING INSTRUCTION

In his book, *Before Stanislavsky*, McTeague (1993) described the history of acting instruction in America. According to McTeague, such training as actors received prior to the 1850s came from their participation in repertory stock companies where they "learned by observing" during their ascent from "apprentice" to "possession of parts" (p. XII). In 1875, Steele MacKaye opened the first American school devoted exclusively to acting: The St. James Theatre School. In subsequent years, he also established, alone or with partners, the Union Square School, the Madison Square School, and the Lyceum School. Dramatic training programs proliferated, and soon the East Coast boasted institutions such as the American Academy of Dramatic Arts, The Emerson College of Oratory, The Stanhope–Wheatcroft School, and The National Dramatic Conservatory. This situation prevailed until approximately 1925, by which time, in McTeague's words, "the vitality of the professional school movement had been inherited by universities and colleges which began competing for the right to train actors" (McTeague, 1993, p. xvi). Soon after this period, college texts on theater started to appear. One of the earliest was John Dolman, Jr.'s (1928), *The Art of Play Production*. In it, Dolman identified the parameters of almost all future discussions of memorization for actors:

There are two distinct methods of memorization, and the answer is not the same for both. By the one method the act of memorizing is made a purely mechanical process having no relation to the study of meaning; the two things are, so to speak, carried on independently by two separate portions of the mind. By the other method the words, actions, and meanings are memorized coordinately, and all associations built up from the start. (Dolman, 1928, pp. 245–246)

The first method, Dolman felt, was best practiced by professionals who knew from experience that they were able to learn mechanically without performing mechanically. The second method had the disadvantage of requiring the actors to spend a large portion of the rehearsal period with book in hand and eye on page, but at least actors could learn meaning, lines, and business so they were coordinated early on. Subsequent authors have opted for one method over the other, but Dolman treated them evenhandedly, although he insisted that the mechanical approach was not for beginners.

In 1938, Franklin and Dixon wrote a text called *Rehearsal* that contained two pages of advice on memorization. Now in its sixth edition, the book's message is highly prescriptive: "Do not attempt to memorize lines apart from the action they accompany. Do not memorize lines without first moving through the action of the play" (p. 86). The authors follow these general instructions with nine specific rules concerning marking of cues, locating of key words, transcribing dialects phonetically, marking meaningful phrases, locating plot lines, reading scenes aloud after every rehearsal to incorporate director's suggestions, integrating sight, sound and movement during memorization, recruiting friends for cuing (including out-of-order cuing), and cultivating general memory skills by attempting to recall all events of the day before retiring each night.

In the late 1940s, as the number of college and university theater departments increased, so did the number of acting texts. In 1947, Cornell University's H. D. Albright wrote *Working up a Part*. In an appendix entitled "Suggestions for Study and Memorization," he advanced the notion that some students are more visual-minded than auditory-minded and that this dichotomy would necessarily affect the usefulness of the devices he outlined. Although Albright did not cite any specific sources for the advice he gave, his suggestions are consistent with a number of psychological learning principles, some dating back to Ebbinghaus (1885/1913). For example, Albright stated:

Carry your memorization well beyond the point necessary for simple recall. If you can barely repeat your lines as you lie back in an easy-chair, without external distraction, then you must certainly expect to break down from time to time under the varied stimuli of a stage rehearsal. (Albright, 1947, p. 128)

Albright also recommended that study sessions should be neither too short nor too long: ½ hour to 2½ hours at a time. In addition, he decried *rote memorization*:

> Do not be deceived by the immediate and tangible results you may achieve by mechanically applying a line-by-line or speech-by-speech method. For most persons this is the long way around. It promises minor results immediately, but it takes longer in the end; and the consequent reading of the lines is likely to be stereotyped and unexpressive. (p. 129)

The memory advice given by Albright included what many psychologists now call *overlearning*, a phenomenon empirically investigated by Ebbinghaus. He found a positive correlation between the number of repetitions and the strength of the memory trace.

In one of the best known of all acting texts, *Acting is Believing*, McGaw (1955) shifted the emphasis from how a role should be learned to when. In McGaw's view, memorization should take place about halfway through the rehearsal process. This, of course, implies that the deep meaning should be learned along with the words. As the author stated, "It is best not to memorize until you have completed your score—until you know your intentions, your physical and verbal actions, your structural units, your subtext, your monologues, your images" (p. 213).

Of the midcentury acting texts, one of the largest sections on memory can be found in *Make Believe—The Art of Acting* by Goodman (1956). Three short chapters, comprising 14 pages, presented a theoretical view, and a later three-page section discussed practical application. Goodman's first chapter on memorization described his understanding of the actor's paradox. He believed that the actor necessarily must think as the character. Because the character is not remembering lines furnished by an author, but speaking words he or she is prompted to use by the nature of the situation, it follows that the character must not remember any performance technicalities. To resolve this paradox, the author suggested a theoretical construct. He did not claim that it was scientifically accurate, just that it made his point clear. Goodman proposed that there were two functions to the human mind: the conscious and the nonconscious. (He avoided the terms unconscious or subconscious to avoid confusion with psychoanalytic theory.) In Goodman's view, the conscious mind of the actor must be solely concerned with what the character wants vis-à-vis the other characters in the dramatic situation, and the nonconscious mind contains all the knowledge the actor possesses about the performance. In Goodman's words:

> And that is the solution of our paradox. That is how the actor can simultaneously remember and not remember technical training, lines, cues, business, and previous rehearsals and performances. All of these and related matters, which are no concern of the character, yet of considerable concern to the actor, the actor must transfer (in

the terms of our figurative explanation) from his conscious to his non-conscious mind, thus leaving his conscious mind free to be occupied by the character's thoughts. (Goodman, 1956, p. 31)

As to how this transfer was accomplished, Goodman (1956) wrote, "Primarily we do it by means of repetition" (p. 32). The author advanced the notion of a mental groove that was deepened with every repetition, providing that repetition is made with full concentration. As with his other constructs, Goodman said the concept was purely figurative, but he felt that the idea of an ever-deepening groove would aid the actor in retaining the lines and other technicalities. This advice would be in line with Ebbinghaus' (1885/1913) finding that repetitions serve to cause the material to be "more or less deeply engraved in some mental substratum" (p. 53). However, like Albright before him, Goodman did not cite sources. Finally, Goodman cautioned actors against quitting when they are "bedroom perfect," but suggested they continue concentrated repetition until there is such complete transference that the cue line elicits the proper response automatically with no conscious thought:

> The association between the cue and your line to follow has become by then what the layman calls "automatic" or "second nature." When you have reached that point, then you have really made the "transference," and understand how an actor can completely make believe he is a character, not thinking, feeling or doing anything which the character would not be thinking, feeling or doing, while retaining in his "non-conscious mind" whatever may be necessary for only the actor to remember. (Goodman, 1956, p. 36)

It is somewhat ironic that Goodman refers to "automatic" as a layman's term, since it is about the only term he uses that can be found in the cognitive literature of today. Whether repetition is an efficient strategy for attaining this automaticity of recall (with hours of verbal material) is discussed later.

Meisner, a revered teacher who was active until his death in February 1997, also suggested that actors should learn by repetition. According to the book *Sanford Meisner on Acting*, his advice to students on memorization was, "I want you to take your script and learn it without meaning, without readings, without interpretation, without anything. Just learn the lines by rote, mechanically" (Meisner & Longwell, 1987, p. 67).

The David Mamet-inspired book, *Practical Handbook for the Actor* (Bruder et al., 1986), echoed this sentiment. The authors stated:

> The best advice we can give you about the lines you will be speaking is to learn them by rote so that you don't have to concentrate on them while you are playing. We've found drilling the lines while jogging or exercising to be effective because it relieves some of the tedium. Memorize the lines without inflection and you will avoid the habit

of line readings—that is, of repeating lines in the same predetermined manner regardless of what is going on in the scene. (Bruder et al., 1986, p. 57)

However, in *Challenge for the Actor*, the highly regarded Broadway actress and teacher Uta Hagen wrote:

> As you make your particularizations, much of what you have to say will become inevitable, and, when followed up in rehearsals by the discovery of your verbal intents and expectations, the words will be further validated until "learning the lines" has become a byproduct of the work, replacing the outmoded method of mechanical memorization. (Hagen, 1991, p. 117)

Because dozens upon dozens of acting texts have been published, it seemed advisable to examine today's most frequently used works in order to gain an accurate view of current role memorization instruction. Therefore, we sent a questionnaire to the acting instructors at the country's 35 largest college and university theater programs. The questionnaire was very brief (two items) to encourage prompt responding. Instructors were asked to identify the acting texts they used and the personal advice they gave regarding role memorization. Thirty responses were received.

WIDELY USED TEXTS

The most popular author was Robert Cohen of the University of California at Irvine with 10 mentions (5 for *Acting Power*, 3 for *Acting One*, and one each for *Acting Professionally* and *Acting in Shakespeare*), followed by Uta Hagen with 7 mentions (5 for *Respect for Acting* and 2 for *A Challenge for the Actor*). The results of this small survey are quite consistent with those of a major 1990–1991 survey in which 610 colleges and universities responded (Aldridge, 1993). While conducted for a completely different purpose, this earlier survey identified the 12 most used acting texts; 10 of the 12 authors were the same as in our own survey, although, in a few cases, represented by other works. However, the diversity in both samples was enormous. In ours, 34 different books were cited and of those, only 12 received more than one mention each.

Throughout the texts, the primary concern was with the actor's imaginative resources. Exercise after exercise was offered for the purpose of developing the actor into a more sensitive emotional "instrument." The primary emphasis was on teaching him or her a viable process for determining what the character wants in the dramatic situation and on how to honestly pursue that want every night on stage. Indeed, virtually every one of the texts subscribed to the notion that good acting consists of living truthfully in imaginary circumstances. A great many of them, including the three seminal works of Stanislavski, *An Actor Prepares* (1936/1984), *Building a Character* (1949/1985), and *Creating a Role* (1961/1983), did not even mention memorization. However, Stanislavski did acknowledge the problem of the dichotomous nature of script learning. His fictional student, Kostya, said, "I had read the text of the role by itself, I had played the character by itself, without relating the one to the other. The words interfered with the acting, and the acting with the words" (Stanislavski, 1936/1984, p. 5). The omission of instruction on memorization is particularly interesting in Stanislavski's case since, in his autobiography, he had confessed that he himself had a memory problem for which he could not find a solution although he had devoted his life to investigating the acting process. In 1924, 18 years after inaugurating the Stanislavski System, he wrote about the dilemma of being out of tune with the text:

> Part of this fault must be blamed on my naturally defective memory. This even forces me to watch myself in the moments of complete spiritual revelation and when I am completely in the grasp of my intuition and emotion. In those moments my memory seems to throw out its buffers, without giving me the opportunity to touch that high point where the region of the superconscious begins. My memory, which distrusts itself, is almost completely devoid of mechanical action, and forces me to watch myself continuously so that I may not break the continuity of the text. Otherwise there would be trouble. There would be a pause, a white blot on the sheet where the words of the part are written, complete helplessness and panic. This great fault takes away from me at least twenty-five percent of my temperament in climacteric [sic] moments. My faulty oral memory is stressed by the fact that in calm scenes and pauses, or during rehearsals, when I speak my own words without having learned the text, I can freely reveal myself at full and show all that is in my soul. (Stanislavski, 1924, p. 228)

In the remaining years of his life, Stanislavski never reported having solved this problem. Indeed, in a subsequent Russian edition of his autobiography (which he revised at the age of 65), he stated that, even at that late point in his life, the retrieval of the words from memory prevented him from surrendering himself completely to intuition and emotion (Stanislavski, 1928). Thus, it appears that the acknowledged master of all acting theorists regarded a faulty verbal memory as a serious defect that could take away 25% of an actor's absorption in a role, yet was basically uncorrectable.

Of the texts in our survey that did address line learning, the subject was usually disposed of in a few paragraphs or, at most, a few pages. Generally, the only specific techniques offered for memory enhancement were to engage in distributed practice and to involve more than one modality by writing out the to-be-remembered material. Otherwise, the advice offered was almost always procedural (such as audiotaping cues in order to efficiently drill lines), although many of the writers emphasized the integration of lines with other aspects of performance such as the characters' motivations. The following section from *The Actor at Work* (Benedetti, 1994) is more or less typical (in terms of the amount of coverage of memorization in modern texts):

> As soon as possible, you will begin to put your book aside so that you can explore the action on your feet. This, of course, requires learning the lines. You will have to find your own best method for line memorization. Some actors like to have a friend read the other parts (cue them); some make a tape recording of their lines to listen to at night; some even write out their lines. Many find it useful to begin working in paraphrase, finding the ideas behind the lines in their own words first.
>
> However you work, learn the action as well as the lines; that is, learn the words in the context of the give-and-take of the scene, paying considerable attention to what the other character is saying in addition to your own responses. This is not only an easier way of learning lines; it also makes learning them a useful first step in your exploration of the action. (Benedetti, 1994, p. 218)

This section constitutes the entire coverage of memory in a book of 268 pages.

One of the most complete sections on memorization can be found in Cohen's *Acting One* (1992). As usual, it starts with procedural advice:

> Begin by underlining or highlighting all your lines. Start reading the text; read aloud for your own part, to yourself for the other character's part. Start with a quarter page or so, and go back to the beginning each time you complete this small section. Soon you will have your first few lines in your memory. Get a postcard or index card and cover your first line. Read (to yourself) the line before it (your cue line), and recite your line from memory. Move the card down and read (to yourself) the next cue line or lines. Recite your next line from memory. Gradually go through the script, an hour or so at a time, lowering the card as you memorize more and more lines; eventually, you will have the text committed to memory. (p. 61)

However, Cohen then added two pages that discussed the mnemonic benefits of association. He advised actors to create relationships between cues and responses, particularly when the responses were nonsequiturs. He recommended that the actor figure out a connection in the character's mind so that the response is really made to a mental cue that is, in turn, a logical response to the actual cue. As an example, he quotes the following exchange from *Who's Afraid of Virginia Wolfe?*

> Nick: And that, of course, would make us cretins.
>
> George: So it would. Tell me about your wife's money. (p. 63)

The second half of George's line is obviously a nonsequitur. Cohen said that the actor playing George might think, "Anybody who would crack a joke like that must be a member of the idle rich" or, alternately, he might picture a cretin counting money (p. 63). Cohen felt that either mental cue would trigger George's reference to money.

One characteristic of all the texts was that the instruction was based totally on what the author's experience led him or her to believe was the most effective procedure. No experimental evidence of that effectiveness was ever offered. In fact, prior to our own research, apparently no scientific attempt was ever made to investigate whether certain script-learning procedures lead to more efficient retention and more effective performance than others.

RESPONSES TO QUESTION TWO

The other item on the questionnaire concerned personal instruction on memorization. Although a number of respondents simply wrote, "None," the following samples indicate the range and variety from those who did respond:

- Just as with the term "stage fright," I rarely speak of memorization. I believe that if the training succeeds in elimination of self-consciousness and provides positive approaches to work on stage, memorizing almost never becomes a "problem."
- While I agree it is easier for actors to learn lines in rehearsal, I actually prefer for actors to learn lines prior to rehearsal, or at least very early in the rehearsal process, so they can interact visually (and emotionally) with the other actors prior to formal blocking. This is because I value actor-interaction and dynamic character relationships somewhat more highly than script (or even motive) "interpretation." I do not make any effort whatsoever to direct or coach the "acting" in my productions, or classes, until lines are fully (and precisely) memorized and the actors have their eyes totally freed from the script. (Reactionary as this may seem.)
- Not to memorize too early.
- In realistic text, lines will come in relation to action and life developed; in elevated (nonrealistic) text, lines should be learned by rote through attention to verbs and operative words.
- Quiet—meaning memorization requires concentration. So, a student has to find quiet in order to apply his or her own method of memorization.
- All work on the text should be done aloud. Silent memorization is deadly—it is your ear and your mouth which must memorize the sense of the speech through the action of speaking.
- As a part of classes and production/rehearsal process, I introduce students to a variety of ideas/choices. Each actor responds to the task of memorization differently. For many it is a matter of their learning styles. An example might be drawn from neuro-linguistic programming (NLP). Some are visual, others auditory or kinesthetic learners and so my suggestions would vary. I might encourage students to draw story-maps, the way writer/storyteller Melissa Bunce does, to aid in their memorization. I might encourage them to read it onto a tape and play it back or to act it out physically in order to learn it.

The most interesting aspect of these personal comments was that, with the very rare exceptions just quoted, the instructors seemed to feel that memorization was largely or even completely incidental to the acting process. As is seen in the next chapter, highly experienced actors appear to have the same view.

2

PSYCHOLOGICAL RESEARCH INTO ACTORS' MENTAL PROCESSES

When we started this series of studies, a search of the memory literature revealed only two experiments concerning acting expertise. The first (Oliver & Ericsson, 1986) investigated the accessibility and speed of retrieval of various parts of a role after the role had been thoroughly learned and was being professionally performed in repertory. Although this study did not address the question of learning strategy, it presented fascinating evidence on the direct accessibility of specific lines from any part of the play with minimal (one- or two-word) probes.

Indeed, there appeared to be only one published experiment that studied actors' encoding processes (Intons-Peterson & Smyth, 1987). However, it did not concern professional expertise; it used undergraduate acting students who had been identified by their department as superior memorizers, and compared their approaches to learning prose passages with those of a general student population. Both groups had to repeat the passages aloud, with or without preliminary reading to learn the gist, and the differences in such factors as the size of the repeated blocks was measured. Thus the strategies professional actors use when working on a role apparently had never been investigated. Therefore, we conducted a pilot study in which we collected verbal reports from professional actors of various ages, styles, background, and training in order to determine what common factors existed between them (Noice, 1992).

THE PILOT STUDY

A prime objective of this study was to identify the underlying processing skill that characterizes the performances of these experts. Nine professional actors were recruited individually, and each was mailed a blank cassette tape. The first two participants received identical instructions asking them to describe the procedures they used in preparing and learning roles. Both actors gave a detailed breakdown of their approach to analysis, preparation, and rehearsal. While a great deal could be inferred from their reports about their memorization processes, they gave very few specifics in this regard and therefore were excluded from the final analysis. Because of this, instructions were reworded, and the remaining seven participants were asked to describe the memorization process they used in the course of learning a role. In order to avoid demand characteristics, no other instructions were given. All participants returned the completed tapes, which were then transcribed.

Analysis

Before listing those points on which there seemed to be general agreement, we emphasize that these verbal reports were not generated while the participants were engaged in the task of learning a role; rather they represented the actors' general approach. However, because the nature of information requested in our protocols was procedural rather than introspective, there is no reason to assume it would be epiphenomenal. As Ericsson and Simon (1993) pointed out, "Whenever verbalizations correspond to plausible intermediate states in a processing model for the problem solving activity, we can plausibly infer that this information is actually used in generating the problem solution" (p. 171).

These protocols were examined for commonalities among participants. Table 2.1 lists the basic approaches that actors claimed they used when learning a role.

The most important finding was that, contrary to the advice of some of the distinguished teachers discussed in the previous chapter, not a single actor reported starting with rote memorization. All seven stressed the importance of identifying the meaning of each line before committing it to memory. While this consensus existed with respect to such concepts as taking the character's perspective or ascribing intentions, individual differences were found regarding the mechanics of studying a role. For example, only three out of seven used a friend or tape recorder for auditory cuing.

Highlights from Protocols

All seven actors stated that they first went through the script many times, trying to extract the deep meaning of the text, before they aimed for word-for-word accuracy. That is, they tried to understand and retain the ideas before trying to memorize how these ideas were expressed. As Actor #7 put it:

> I pretty much learn the ideas first, before I really care about the exact words...after all that's what we're doing here, exchanging ideas...we're imitating life after all. That

seems to be the way it works in life, you know. Somebody throws an idea at you and you throw an idea back at them. (Noice, 1992, p. 419)

As a matter of fact, many stated explicitly that they make an effort not to learn any of the words prior to rehearsal. Actor #3 explained:

TABLE 2.1

Factors Involved in the Memorization of Theatrical Roles

A. Statements indicating no intent to memorize until other procedures have been accomplished

Task	# of Actors (out of 7) Mentioning This Item
1. Read play many times before any memorizing	7
2. Learn lines generally after blocking	7
3. Use a procedure not based on rote repetition	7
4. Pick-up lines while rehearsing with other actors	4
5. Paraphrase first, learn exact words later	3
6. Divide a role into sections and learn those	2

B. Statements concerned with motivations, intentions, or interactions of characters

Task	# of Actors (out of 7) Mentioning This Item
1. Consider character's growth or progress in play	7
2. Associate motivation with blocking	7
3. Study character's ideas before learning lines	7
4. Think about relations with other characters	5
5. Analyze character's motivations	3

C. Statements regarding technical aspects of role learning

Task	# of Actors (out of 7) Mentioning This Item
1. Use of friend or tape recorder for cuing	3
2. Reproducing lines exactly as written	3
3. Writing out long speeches	2
4. Picturing the way the page looks	2
5. Learning progression of events in play	2

Note. From "Elaborative Memory Strategies of Professional Actors," by H. Noice, 1992, *Applied Cognitive Psychology*, 6(5), p. 420. Copyright © 1992 by John Wiley. Adapted with permission.

> Now one of the things I don't want to do as an actor is memorize the lines out loud in a certain rote fashion, so that I say them the same way every time. It would be faster—it is faster to just memorize all the words rotely out loud. But that—you don't want to do that. (p.419)

Actor #4 concurred:

> What I don't do: I don't memorize right away. And, in fact, if I have a problem, it's in keeping myself from memorizing too soon. Most of the time I memorize by magic—and that is I don't really memorize. There is no effort involved. There seems to be no process involved: It just happens. One day early on, I know the lines. (Noice, 1992, p. 420)

In general, the actors said they read the script the first time to extract the story line, but on second reading, they tried to discover the personalities of the characters they were portraying. This problem-solving process seemed to involve posing a number of questions such as: What does my character want? What does my character *do* to obtain it? How does my character think and feel? Why does my character act in certain ways? As Actor #7 put it, "trying to find out the whys" (Noice, 1992, p. 420). This participant further described the process as a form of backward chaining:

> We do things in reverse in the theater. We get the script which is…at the end of the thought process: We have the lines there. Normally in life, you have an impulse and then a thought which you put into words. Well, I have the words, I get the words first in this finished script. And so I have to go back and find out what the thought was, to have you say those words. And more importantly, what was the impulse that created the thought that created the words, and usually it could be an emotional kind of thing. What is the reason for that thought? That's the way I have always thought of it. (pp. 420–421)

As Actor #9 pointed out:

> I have to figure out how she goes about getting what she wants. Now, of course, a lot of times the character doesn't get what he wants but you have to play the [psychological] action; an action to get what you want. Every character, in every play, I think, is trying to find something. So you have to put those in doable verb terms…."I want to make him apologize." (Noice, 1992, p. 421)

This emphasis on psychological action was apparent in the other protocols as well. A number of participants stated that they didn't try to remember the words but the actions or the thoughts that produced the actions. Actor #6 put it this way:

> I memorize not the words I'm saying but the thought process that's going on in the scene. I hear somebody asking me something or requesting something of me and

logically I say the following thing. It's me responding to something someone has asked of me or is saying to me (p. 421).

Actor #9 agreed that he tried to remember the reason for saying a particular line and that often this line was said in direct response to a question. He explained, "The line for me needs to grow out of what the other person is doing"(p. 421).

It appears that what this participant memorizes is what the other person said that caused him to say those particular words. Discovering the intentions that prompted an action seems to be an integral part of a professional actor's approach to studying a role. All nine actors expressed the thought that before learning any of the lines, they tried to discern a character's intentions. Although they used different terms, such as goals or actions or motivations or "figuring out the whys," all of them reported that they analyzed a play from the standpoint of what the character is hoping to accomplish.

Dividing a play or a scene by objectives seems to give it structure. According to Actor #3, each objective functions as a chunk. As he put it, "A role is a whole thing. It's a person who starts at one place, goes to X events and ends up in another place. You do learn it by segments ... and then the memorization is easier" (Noice, 1992, p. 421).

Not surprisingly, all actors were concerned about being able to create an emotional reality on stage. In their view, that is much harder than memorizing the words. Many of them explicitly stated that these emotions are memorized as well because, according to Actor #7:

> Something has to be going on underneath before you say the line in most cases. The lead female over here is doing a monologue which is making me angry. So that is something that has to be memorized too, isn't it? I have to remember...yes, making me angry—and it's a page and a half before I even say anything. So, anyway...that's part of the play too, isn't it? (Noice, 1992, pp. 421–422)

All of the actors also made a point of emphasizing that they never learned their lines until they learned the blocking (the movements and physical business on stage) and that this helped them retrieve the appropriate lines. Actor #2 said, "It does help to know where you're going when you're learning your lines. If I remembered, ok, I get up here, I go to the chair, I set down my glass, the lines come with it."Or in the words of Actor #3, "the movement is a lot for the memorization...if the blocking is good, then emotionally the words are right. So that when you move in a certain kind of way, it becomes natural to say those kinds of words" (Noice, 1992, p. 422).

Actor #4 stressed that he never memorizes any lines prior to having learned the blocking. He said:

> You've got to have these two tracks going simultaneously, this is what I say and this is when and where I move. If they're somehow joined together and they get put in at the same time, one feeds the other, and you move and say the line. (Noice, 1992, p. 422)

Although many of the actors specifically mentioned that they did try to learn the lines exactly as the playwright had written them, none of them expressed any difficulty with accomplishing that task. Most of their effort seemed to be focused on making that character they're portraying real and believable. Actor #4 expressed it as follows:

> This has been an interesting process for me, this memorizing a part—because it isn't words. The actor creates all that stuff that's underneath the words, and the words are just the topping, the words are the froth on top of the beer. The actor has to create the mug, and the hops and the beer and the fermentation and all of that; and when that happens, the foam just gets there—by some natural 'blump'. It's just there. It just happens. (Noice, 1992, p. 422)

AN EXAMPLE OF ROLE PREPARATION

Although all the actors stressed analyzing before memorizing, none of them gave a step-by-step example of how this analysis was applied to a particular role. Therefore, one additional actor was recruited who was asked to both outline his method of analysis and to supply an example of the preparation with a specific role he had played. The actor's verbal protocol is shown in the form of diagrams in Figs. 2.1 and 2.2.

As shown in Fig. 2.1, the actor apparently organized the text in a hierarchical fashion: The top node is occupied by the superobjective, or the main goal that the actor believes the character would be pursuing for most of his life. The next level contains the main objective the character is pursuing during the time period covered in the play, and the level just below consists of each major objective the character tries to achieve each time he appears upon the scene.

The actor stated that each major objective is composed of a great many individual smaller action patterns, called beats. He defined beats as the smallest unit of goal-directed action. A character does something to attain an immediate goal; that is, he commits an action and someone else reacts to it, which, in turn, evokes another action, and so forth until the character succeeds or fails to reach the immediate goal. This resolution leads to his attempt to reach the goal of the next beat, and so on. These beats occupy the lowest level.

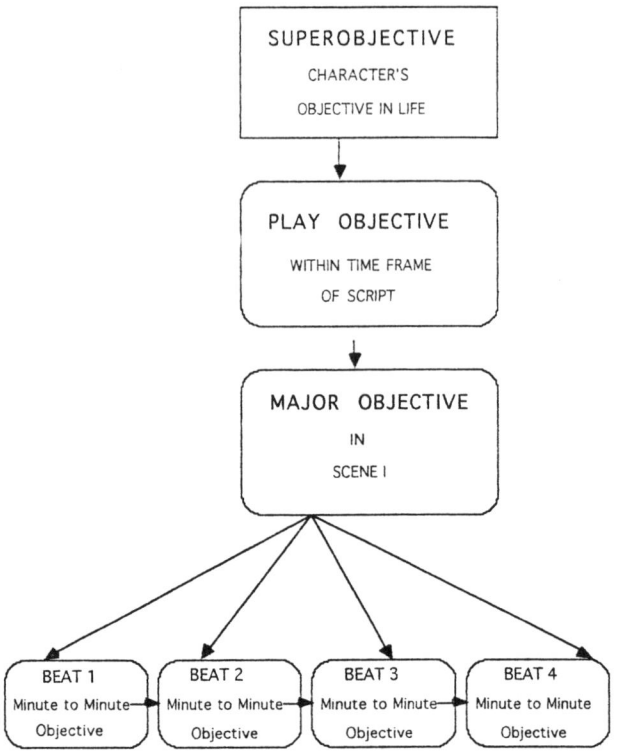

FIG. 2.1. Preparation of a scene from a contemporary play. *Note.* From "Elaborative Memory Strategies of Professional Actors," by H. Noice, 1992, *Applied Cognitive Psychology, 6*(5), p. 423. Copyright © 1992 by John Wiley. Reprinted with permission.

An example of how the actor reported to have scored the role of Victor Velasco in Neil Simon's play *Barefoot in the Park* is shown in Fig. 2.2. Each of the slots has been instantiated with the events of the text.

Thus, it appears that this actor's strategy in learning a role consisted of recognizing the assigned character's overall plan and also recognizing that a scene consists of a series of subgoals (Beats 1–4) each of which must be accomplished in turn before the overall plan can succeed.

CONCLUSION

It is obvious that actors do not consider themselves expert memorizers as such; rather they are expert recreators of reality. Verbatim retention appears to be a byproduct of the strategy the actor uses to create the sense of reality in each ongoing moment. The actor determines what the character would be thinking when using those particular words, and this in-depth understanding of the underlying thought allows the actor to do his real job of making the performance new each night.

It is an intriguing finding that a strategy not directed toward memorization results in verbatim retention. It has long been shown that elaboration leads to improved recall (e.g., Craik & Tulving, 1975) and that its effectiveness is dependent on how precisely it elaborates the meaning of the to-be-remembered sentence (Stein & Bransford, 1979). However, what appears to be new here is that a strategy based on embellishing the text rather than memorizing it nevertheless leads to word-for-word recall. A possible explanation is that actors repeatedly read the script to ascertain how the character's plan is furthered by those exact words. As a result, the words become indexed to the plan. When the actor retrieves the plan, the exact words that are indexed to the plan are also retrieved even though they were never intentionally memorized. This would explain such typical actor comments as, "the words just seemed to be there," and "I memorize by magic."

This interpretation is in keeping with the comments found in almost all of the reports, comments that indicate that actors create highly detailed elaborative networks in which every line is turned into a goal statement.

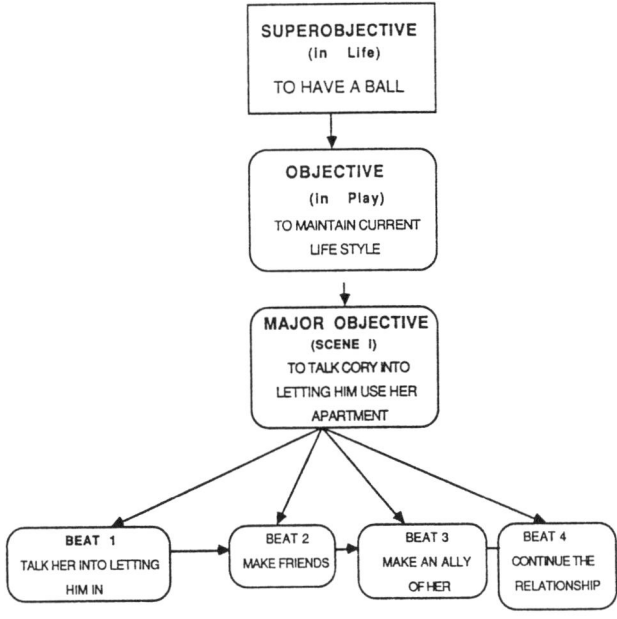

FIG. 2.2. How one actor represents a specific role. *Note.* From "Elaborative Memory Strategies of Professional Actors," by H. Noice, 1992, *Applied Cognitive Psychology,* 6(5), p. 424. Copyright © 1992 by John Wiley. Reprinted with permission.

Apparently this deep elaboration is at least partially responsible for the phenomenal amount of complex material retained without line-by-line memorization. However, this pilot study did not set out to investigate the exact nature of the elaborations actors generate, or to determine the contribution of expertise to the generation of those elaborations, or to provide evidence for the memory benefits of such a process. To answer those questions, we turn to experimental inquiry. These investigations are described in subsequent chapters.

3

Experimental Investigation of Actors' Learning Strategies

In those relatively rare instances when verbatim retention of theatrical roles has been addressed in the cognitive literature, it has almost always been assumed that roles are memorized by rote (e.g., Hasher & Griffin, 1978; see also Ebbinghaus, 1885/1913). However, no indication of this approach was found in our pilot study. Therefore, this experiment (Noice, 1991) investigated the possibility that actors may have a strategy that is much more efficient than rote memorization yet yields verbatim results.

Many studies have examined recognition of verbatim details of spoken discourse. One such study (Kintsch & Bates, 1977) showed that 48 hours after a normal classroom lecture that contained no mention of a subsequent memory test, participants recognized the differences between verbatim statements and paraphrases of topic sentences, details, and extraneous remarks. After a 5-day delay, the students could no longer recognize verbatim topic statements or detail statements but still showed good recognition for extraneous remarks.

Keenan, MacWhinney, and Mayhew (1977) tested verbatim recognition of conversation by recording a luncheon discussion at the University of Denver. Although no hint was given that participants would be tested, 30 hours later they showed significant recognition memory for statements that contained wit, sarcasm, humor, personal criticism, and figures of speech, (e.g., "If in Madagascar they're weird enough to put the verb first, you can guess what their eye movements must be like," p. 552). Keenan et al. concluded that those statements recognized as being verbatim were those that were concerned with the intentions of the speaker and were phrased in a colorful and interesting way.

Using both recognition tasks and free recall, Hjelmquist and his colleagues (e.g., Hjelmquist, 1984; Hjelmquist & Gidlund, 1985) also found considerable verbatim memory for live conversation and further found that, during delayed free recall, the participants demonstrated greater verbatim memory for their own utterances than for the utterances of the questioner (Hjelmquist & Gidlund, 1985).

Taken together, these studies suggest that personal, live, colorful conversation has a high degree of memorability, particularly for utterances of the speaker. As is later shown, actors, in the course of learning a role, consistently embellish it with these easy-to-remember qualities.

SKILLED MEMORY THEORY

The approach that the actors in the pilot study appeared to be using was far different from the approaches generally found to be effective for intentional memorization. Chase and Ericsson (1982) reported on the strategy developed by a digit span expert, SF, who in the course of 100 training sessions developed a mnemonic system for remembering over 80 digits. To explain the superior performance of SF and other experts in different fields, Chase and Ericsson proposed *Skilled Memory theory*, which suggests three principles common to expert memory in a variety of domains.

1. Experts organize material efficiently so that working memory can hold extremely large chunks of information.
2. Experts' specialized knowledge allows material to be encoded in a form that facilitates retrieval.
3. Practice enables experts to recognize and encode patterns with great efficiency. Therefore, large amounts of information can be processed quickly.

The question is whether these same factors lie behind the ease with which many professional actors learn roles. It is one central thesis of this book that actors' role-learning processes do involve these three aspects of Skilled Memory theory, but that they are brought into play indirectly by a strategy based on exploration, not intentional memorization.

Various types of tasks have been used in the course of testing skilled memory. One type involves a task where the goal is intentional memorization (e.g., remembering digits, Chase & Ericsson, 1982; remembering restaurant orders, Ericsson & Polson, 1988). Another type involves a task where the goal is not intentional memorization but for which expert memory is indispensable for performance of the task (e.g., performing mental calculations requires holding large subtotals in memory, Staszewski, 1988).

This experiment concerns a third type, in which the task does not involve retention of material at all, only analysis. Conversations with various New York and regional theatre actors indicate that they use the identical analytical approach whether the role is to be eventually performed from memory or not. That is, they use the same preparation strategy for a situation where they read the lines (radio plays, auditions, concert readings, etc.) as when they perform on stage from memory. Yet over the course of rehearsal for a stage play, this strategy apparently leads to verbatim retention. The information gained from acting texts, acting instructors' comments, and from the statements of the actors themselves indicates that the initial study of a playscript consists of what many researchers call *plan recognition* (e.g., Schmidt, 1976; Schmidt, Sridharan, & Goodson, 1978) during which the actions of characters are explained by inferring the goals they are pursuing. We surmised that actors, in order to do this, must elaborate on the text, speculating on the motivations that prompted the dialogue, and, as a result, acquire a memory representation that is far richer and more detailed than the text itself. An extension of this reasoning indicates that the richness of the memory representation that has been constructed of the text could be inferred by determining the number and types of embellishments generated by actors during their initial studying of the script. In order to investigate this issue, we devised three different tasks, each designed to examine a different aspect of an actor's retention of a role. Because each task generated its own data, only the first is discussed in this chapter; the others are described in subsequent chapters.

THE ELABORATED RECALL TASK

Rationale

Two main questions were addressed by this first task:

1. Can the process that actors claim allows them to retain large portions of the script without line-by-line memorization be experimentally verified and specified? If, during comprehension, actors actively ask questions in order to provide explanations for the actions of the characters, then many of these explanations should also be included in their recall protocols. To investigate this issue, experts and novices studied the same scene from a play; they then performed a recall test during which they wrote down not only all the actual lines they remembered, but any accompanying thoughts they had had while studying the script.

2. Will the actors' explanatory statements be made predominantly from the perspectives of their assigned characters? It has been shown that taking on the perspective of one of the characters in a narrative has a powerful effect on the organization and retention of material (e.g., Albrecht, O'Brien, Mason, & Myers, 1995; Anderson & Pichert, 1978; Black, Turner, & Bower, 1979; Bower & Morrow, 1990; O'Brien & Albrecht, 1992; Owens, Bower, & Black, 1979). If actors assume the perspectives of their assigned characters, then they should be looking for those traits the assigned characters possess that motivate them to conceive and implement particular plans. Furthermore, evidence of this search should be found in their protocols.

Because the main purpose of this task was to discover the nature of actors' mental processes during script study, the design differed from many expert–novice experiments. The pilot data had shown that actors appear unconcerned with memorization in the course of working on the script. They feel that remembering their lines is analogous to driving to the theater: necessary to get the job done but completely incidental to the work itself.

The experiment was designed to insure that it would uncover the strategies actors actually use in the initial stages of working on the script. Therefore, we decided not to use online protocols in order to avoid introducing any element that might prevent actors from employing their natural strategy. For the same reason, the text was not presented on a computer screen; participants were given typewritten scripts in the standard professional format and told to work on the material as if preparing for an audition. Following a 20-minute study period, participants were asked to recall everything they could of both the script itself and the ideas they generated during study. Of course, the possibility exists that even though the instructions emphasized writing down only those ideas the participant recalled from the study period, some elaborations may have been generated during recall. However, because the purpose of this experiment was to specify the nature of actors' elaborations, determining the specific processing stage was not considered as important as avoiding any procedure that might inhibit the use of the actors' natural strategy. Having obtained these data in a naturalistic setting, we later employed online, think-aloud protocols (chaps. 6 and 7).

Design of the Study

Twenty-eight professional actors (13 males and 15 females) and 28 undergraduate psychology students with no theatrical background (10 males and 18 females) participated in the experiment. No one in either group was familiar with the material used in the experiment.

Fourteen participants served in each cell of a 2 x 2 factorial design with two between-subjects factors: expertise (actors vs. novices) and strategy (gist vs. rote). The first factor was whether the participant belonged to an expert or novice group; the second factor was whether the participant was instructed to study the script using a gist or rote strategy.

The experimental passage was a short scene (about five manuscript pages) for two actors from the play *The Second Man* by S. N. Behrman (1952). It was chosen because it was internally cohesive and therefore intelligible out of context. In addition, the subject matter, love, was thought to be of equal interest to novices and experts, and both groups were assumed to possess about equal amounts of knowledge on the subject. Furthermore, the play is rarely performed today, so the chance of a participant having seen or read it was remote.

Playscripts differ from normal prose in that scripts typically contain fragmentary responses, cut speeches, and parenthetical adjectives that describe the attitude of the speaker. So for purposes of analysis, the script was divided into idea units (based on work by Johnson, 1970). We considered, as one idea unit, any group of words expressing a single thought. Thus the sentence "Wouldn't it be nice if people were like molecules or electrons or whatever you work with?" was one idea unit, as was the phrase "She told me to go home alone." The parts of both actors were approximately the same length (45 idea units for one character and 41 for the other), neither part contained long speeches, and the resolution of the scene was not explicitly stated so it would have to be inferred.

The dominant style of the play is *realistic*, characterized by the attempt to approximate real life on stage. The situation is one the audience accepts as plausible, and the characters act on motivations the audiences accept as true to life. The copy of the scene given to the participants was not divided into idea units but was in normal professional format. (This scene appears in Appendix A.)

Three booklets were prepared. The first consisted of the scene itself preceded by instructions concerning the nature of the task. A second booklet contained a distractor task followed by the elaborated recall task. (The third booklet concerned the cued recall and summarization tasks described in future chapters.) Experts and novices were assigned randomly to one of the two treatment conditions and were tested individually.

Rote Instructions. Participants in this condition (in both the novice and expert groups) were told to memorize their lines by rote repetition (the role of Austin for male participants and the role of Kendall for female participants). They were instructed not to "look ahead or back" but to keep the script covered with a supplied cardboard which contained a window that only exposed one section of the script at a time. (This procedure is similar to one used by Cofer, 1941.)

These instructions prevented, as much as possible, the participants' inadvertent use of meaningful analysis that could have taken place if the participants had been allowed to keep going back to the beginning of the script. The procedure was designed to influence the participant to employ rote learning as frequently defined in the cognitive literature. For example, "learning due to the sheer repetition of something with little contribution from any meaningful or semantic analysis" (Zechmeister & Nyberg, 1982, p. 54). Of course, 100% rote learning is not possible with meaningful material; even learning nonsense syllables may involve some additional mnemonic devices. But our procedure did put strong emphasis on learning purely by repeating.

Following a 2-minute practice session (using a fragment of a different play), participants were instructed to cover the first page of the script with the template and proceed. Participants' study was monitored to insure compliance with experimenter's instruction. The experimenter kept time and adjusted the number of repetitions (adding repetitions for participants who spoke quickly and eliminating repetitions for participants who spoke slowly) in order to get through the entire scene in the allotted time of 20 minutes. While participants were told to memorize, they were not specifically told there would be a recall test.

Gist Instructions. Actors were told to study the scene as if they had to audition for the designated role and that they would have 20 minutes to prepare. They were not told to memorize nor were they informed that there would be a subsequent memory test. Students received the identical instructions except that the phrase "try out" was substituted for "audition" because the former term is almost universally used in colleges and universities.

After 20 minutes of study, participants in all conditions were given a 2-minute distractor task, followed by an elaborated recall task. For the latter, they were given sheets of papers, blank except for a line down the center and the headings, Column A and Column B. Participants were instructed to write down any lines they recalled from the script in any order in Column A and any accompanying thoughts in Column B. No time limit was imposed, but participants were cautioned that Column B entries must be restricted to thoughts they had during the initial 20-minute study period.

Scoring

Column A Utterances. The recalled lines of dialogue were divided into idea units and credit was given for each unit present, regardless of whether the recall was verbatim or paraphrased. If participants, in addition to their assigned lines, also recalled lines of the other character, these were scored separately. Any material that had not been stated in the text was scored as an intrusion. Because, in this task, we were primarily interested in the elaborations that participants generated, the main purpose of the Column A entries was to serve as references for those elaborations reported in Column B.

Column B Utterances. After reading the protocols repeatedly to detect similarities of purpose or expression, it was apparent that all statements fell into one of two categories: explanatory or nonexplanatory. Explanatory statements were further divided into: (a) characterizations, (b) interactions, or (c) externals. (If an utterance served to describe a character in terms of either physical or personality traits, that utterance was scored as a *characterization*; if an utterance described how one character influenced or was influenced by the other character, it was scored as an *interaction*; and if an utterance was concerned with technical aspects of the performance, such as wardrobe, dialects, or specific words to stress, then it was considered an *external*.) Illustrative examples are presented in Table 3.1.

All explanatory elaborations fell into one of the three categories. In most cases, an actor simply gave a straightforward explanation of his or her elaboration as if to describe it to others, but one particular variation in expression stood out, resulting in the creation of a subcategory of interaction: *silent speech*. Here, instead of describing the nature of the interaction, the actor actually wrote out the thought that the character would be thinking while speaking the line; (e. g., the line was, "Are you going to marry him?" The actor elaborated by writing out the underlying thought, "Please say yes.")

Nonexplanatory statements were divided into two categories: (a) editorial comments about the experiment itself, and (b) restatements of scene content without elaboration. Statements that were illegible or contained too little information to be classified were scored as *ambiguous*.

Reliability of Coding. All utterances were coded by one judge (the experimenter). A randomly selected subset consisting of 36 protocols was scored by two independent raters who were blind with respect to the participant's group or condition. Agreement between the judges was virtually unanimous (ranging from .98 for explanatory vs. nonexplanatory comments to 1.0 for characterization vs. externals). The only exception was silent speech vs. interaction with .88. However, as pointed out earlier, silent speech is not a separate category, but an elaborative device used by many actors to express how their character interacts with other characters or with the given situation. Thus, by definition, any verbal utterance coded as silent speech was also an interaction. Although these two categories were

TABLE 3.1

Illustrative Examples of Elaborations by Category Type

Category Type	*Examples*
Interaction	Trying to calm him.
Characterization	Kendall is tough—worldly wise.
Externals	I wonder if I could use an English accent.
Editorial Comment	I felt stupid repeating this.
Restatement of Scene Content	They proceed to talk about how they feel about Monica and Storey.

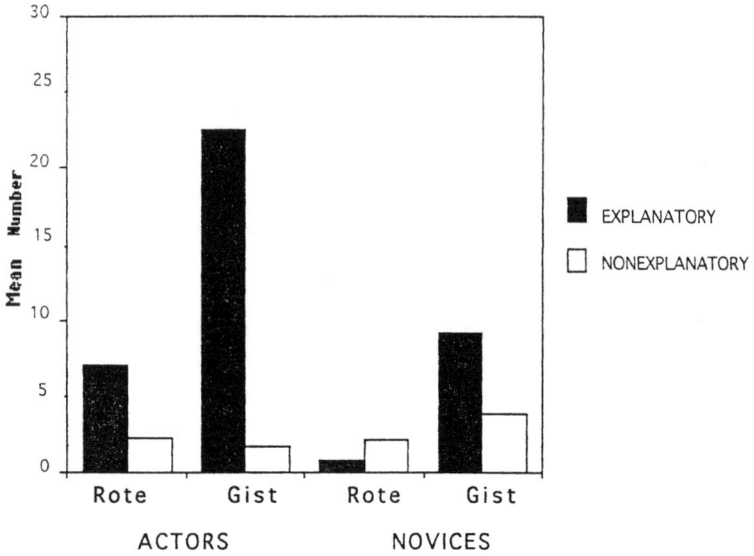

FIG. 3.1. Mean number of utterances generated by actors and novices classified as either explanatory or nonexplanatory statements. From "The Role of Explanations and Plan Recognition in the Learning of Theatrical Scripts," by H. Noice, 1991, *Cognitive Science, 15*, p. 440. Copyright © 1991 by Ablex Publishing Corporation. Reprinted with permission.

not mutually exclusive, they were treated as such so that the interrater agreement could be calculated for interactions phrased as silent speech versus interactions described directly. Even though these both performed the same function, the difference in phrasing was so salient that this interrater agreement of .88 was achieved. Disagreements were resolved through discussion.

Differences Between Experts and Novices

Idea units in each category were tabulated for each participant. The first major question was whether actors constructed more explanatory elaborations than novices. These data are presented in Fig. 3.1. The main finding was the large number of elaborations produced by the actors in the gist condition compared to participants in the rote condition, $t(26) = 3.47$, $p < .01$, confirming our hypothesis that professional actors' memory representations consist not only of the events mentioned explicitly in the text, but also of the explanations generated while reading about those events.

Further inspection of the data showed that not only did actors in the gist condition produce the most explanatory comments, they also reported the fewest number of nonexplanatory comments, $t(26) = 2.02, p < .05$. These patterns of results were consistent with the prediction that one component of an actor's expertise is generation of a large number of explanatory elaborations. (The ratio of actors' explanatory to non-explanatory comments amounted to over 13:1, compared to the novices' ratio of approximately 2:1.)

Next, for each participant, difference scores between the number of explanatory and nonexplanatory statements were computed. These data were then submitted to an analysis of variance with two between-subjects factors (expertise and strategy). There was a statistically significant interaction of expertise with strategy, $F(1, 52) = 5.10, p < .05, MSe = 80.87$. An analysis of simple main effects indicated that use of a gist strategy increased the amount of elaboration, $F(1, 52) = 13.26, p < .01, MSe = 80.67$; but this was not the case for novices, $F(1, 52) = 1.91, p > .05$. A significant main effect of strategy emerged, $F(1, 52) = 25.23, p < .001, MSe = 80.87$ that underscored the fact that participants in the gist condition tended to engage in more explaining than participants in the rote condition.

A second analysis was carried out to determine whether the results would also hold for individual participants. For each of the four conditions, it was assessed how many of the 14 participants had generated more explanatory than nonexplanatory comments. The results showed that every actor in the gist condition and 10 actors in the rote condition produced more explanatory than nonexplanatory comments. However, with novices, 9 participants in the gist condition and only one in the rote condition produced more explanatory than nonexplanatory comments. A chi-square test for independence indicated that there was a significant relationship between expertise and the production of a majority of explanatory comments, $X^2 (1, N = 56) = 14.67, p < .01$. This type of analysis was carried out for each dependent measure and, as here, showed that the results held for individual participants. Therefore, subsequent analyses for individual participants are not reported.

Another major area of interest was the nature of any qualitative differences in the types of elaborations generated by actors and novices. Mean scores were computed for each of the three categories of explanatory elaborations: interactions, characterizations, and externals, plus one subcategory of interaction: silent speech. (Because, as already pointed out, silent speech does not exist by itself but is a particular way of phrasing an interaction, all such utterances were counted as both silent speech and interaction.) These data are presented in Fig. 3.2.

The most obvious difference was in the mean number of utterances that were classified as interactions, $t(54) = 2.80, p < .01$. Interactions constitute the most significant form of elaboration because they capture the essential

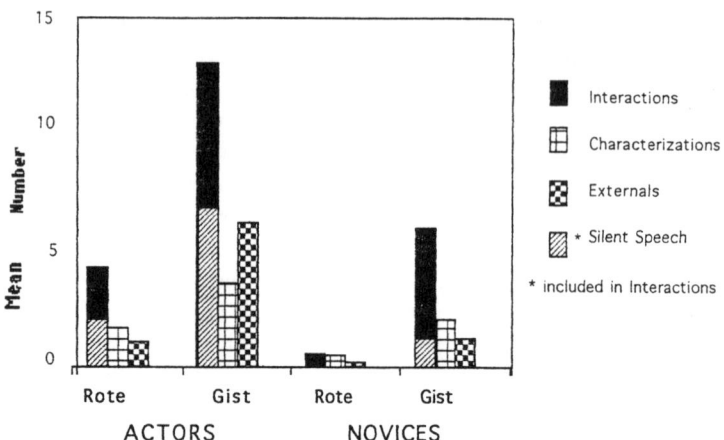

FIG. 3.2. Type of explanatory comments generated by actors and novices as a function of strategy. From "The Role of Explanations and Plan Recognition in the Learning of Theatrical Scripts," by H. Noice, 1991, *Cognitive Science, 15*, p. 441. Copyright © 1991 by Ablex Publishing Corporation. Reprinted with permission.

causality in the play by analyzing how one actor affects or is affected by another, thus causing a change in the relationship or situation. An example of this type of utterance would be: "Kendall finds this man elusive and interesting and is glad for the chance to talk to him alone."

The next category concerned characterizations. On average, participants in both groups produced considerably fewer statements describing stable dispositional properties than statements describing interactions. That is, participants were less prone to say, "He is very honest" than, "He wants her to tell him the truth." In addition, not surprisingly actors in the gist condition generated far more verbal utterances classified as externals than actors in the rote condition, $t(26) = 2.58, p < .05$.

Also, the type of elaboration we called silent speech was used almost exclusively by actors, $t(54) = 2.76, p < .01$. For example, one actress, referring to the line, "I'm glad you came. It was lonesome," elaborated by adding, "I want to get to know him." In this case, her silent speech represents the actress' recognition of Kendall's plan to use this chitchat to get closer to Austin.

Perspective

The other main question was whether participants differed with respect to adopting the perspective of the assigned character. In order to determine this, utterances were scored along another dimension: *Referent* versus *Mental or Emotional Activity*. To be listed under the former, the utterance had to be a statement *about* the character. To be listed under the latter, the utterance had to have described specific mental or emotional activity *by* the character. In other words, the former viewed the character from the outside and the latter viewed the character from the inside. An example of an utterance that would be classified as Referent would be, "Kendall is witty." An example of a statement indicating the presence of Mental or Emotional Activity would be, "Kendall is surprised that she is touched emotionally by a relationship she thought was purely physical." When this activity was present, the rater listed it as "same" (assigned character), "different" (other character), or "both." These data are shown in Table 3.2, together with the results of the independent samples *t*-tests used to analyze the data.

Significant differences between the experimental conditions were observed. Actors in the gist condition by far exceeded all other participants in terms of the number of elaborations generated that were consistent with the perspective of the assigned character, $t(26) = 3.52$, $p < .01$. However, novices in the gist condition did use far more perspective taking than novices in the rote

TABLE 3.2

Mean Number of Explanatory and Nonexplanatory Statements Consistent With Assigned Character's Point of View

Mental or Emotional Activity: (Who is thinking the thought or experiencing the emotion?)

Category	Actors		Novices	
	Rote	Gist	Rote	Gist
Same character	3.6	12.9**	0.3	4.4*
Different character	0.3	0.4	0.2	0.7
Both characters	0	0.1	0	0.4
Total	3.9	13.4	0.5	5.5

Referent: (Who is being talked about?)

Category	Actors		Novices	
	Rote	Gist	Rote	Gist
Same character	1.7	3.5	0.9	2.9
Different character	0.1	0.6	0.6	1.6
Both characters	0.4	0.7	0.1	0.6
Total	2.2	2.8	1.6	5.1
Others (incl. externals)	4.9	6.6	1.3	3.6
Grand Total	11.0	24.8**	3.4	14.3*

Note. By independent *t*-tests: *$p < .01$, within-group comparisons.**$p < .05$, between gist conditions comparison. From "The Role of Explanations and Plan Recognition in the Learning of Theatrical Scripts," by H. Noice, 1991, *Cognitive Science, 15*, p. 443. Copyright © 1991 by Ablex Publishing Corporation. Reprinted with permission.

condition, $t(26) = 2.81, p < .01$. This appears to indicate that the high degree to which actors indulge in perspective-taking is due to their expertise; nevertheless, some perspective-taking is a component of the understanding process itself.

The ratio of statements by actors who viewed their character from the inside as opposed to from the outside was 3.7 to 1, whereas with novices the ratio was 1.5 to 1. Furthermore, one can assess the tendency to view all the characters from the inside as opposed to the outside by comparing the combined figures for same, different and both. This procedure yielded a ratio of 3 to 1 for actors as opposed to 1 to 1 for novices, indicating that, unlike actors, novices were equally likely to view the characters from inside or outside.

For each participant, difference scores between the number of statements describing specific mental or emotional activity by the character and statements about the character were computed. These data were then submitted to an analysis of variance with two between-subjects factors (expertise and strategy). There was a statistically significant interaction of expertise with strategy, $F(1, 52) = 3.94, p < .05, MSe = 826.85$. An analysis of simple main effects indicated that use of a gist strategy appeared to encourage actors to view the character from the inside $F(1, 52) = 14.95, p < .01, MSe = 26.85$, but not novices, $F(1, 52) = 1.12, p > .05, MSe = 26.85$. Significant main effects of expertise and strategy emerged: Actors produced more elaborations that focused on mental or emotional activities of their assigned character than did novices, $F(1, 52) = 13.98, p < .001$; also all participants using a gist strategy focused more on such activities compared to participants using a rote strategy, $F(1, 52) = 12.12, p < .01$.

Extent of Mental Representation

One way to investigate the extent of the detail in the mental representation that participants formed of the text was to compute the total number of actual lines recalled (either verbatim or paraphrased), as well as the accompanying thoughts (explanatory and/or nonexplanatory). These data are represented in Table 3.3 along with the results of the significance tests on the difference between means. Even though the instructions emphasized studying the lines of the assigned character, a few participants recalled some lines of the other character as well. These, plus any intrusions, were scored separately and are also represented in Table 3.3.

As can be seen, both actors and students, when using a rote strategy, recalled fewer actual lines, $t(54) = -4.76, p < .001$ and generated fewer elaborations, $t(54) = -4.77, p < .001$. Of the participants using a gist strategy, the actors generated more elaborations, $t(26) = 2.72, p < .05$, but recalled about the same number of lines of dialogue of the assigned character as novices, $t(26) = -1.36, p > .05$. However, novices recalled more lines of the other character $t(26) = 2.40, p < .05$, so total literal recall of novices was greater, $t(26) = 2.27, p <$

TABLE 3.3

Mean Number of Lines and Accompanying Thoughts Recalled by Actors and Novices as a Function of Strategy

Category	Actors		Novices	
	Rote	Gist	Rote	Gist
Lines recalled				
Assigned character	10.07	15.57	8.21	20.43*
Other character	0.79	1.93	1.29	6.43**
Intrusions	0.29	0.43	0.64	0.64
Total	11.15	17.93*	10.14	27.50**
Thoughts recalled	10.86	24.69**	3.43	14.30*
Grand total	22.01	42.72*	13.57	41.80*

Note. Independent t-tests: *$p < .05$, within-group comparisons. **$p < .05$, between gist conditions comparison. From "The Role of Explanations and Plan Recognition in the Learning of Theatrical

.05. There were no significant differences in the overall recall (literal recall plus elaborations) of the two groups, $t(26) = .16, p > .05$.

AUGMENTED GIST CONDITION

One possible explanation for the results is that actors and novices interpreted the task differently and therefore adopted different strategies. That is, all professional actors know they do not have to memorize their lines for an audition but that a script is available. Consequently, they could put all of their emphasis on elaborating each line. On the other hand, novices would not have this knowledge and might possibly believe that, during an audition, lines had to be recited from memory. Therefore, they might have spent the allotted study time memorizing their lines. Thus, the higher number of elaborations generated by actors and the higher number of total lines recalled from the script by novices could possibly be attributed to strategic differences rather than to different study skills associated with expertise. To assess this possibility, an additional group of novices was tested under conditions identical to those of the previous gist condition but with revised instructions in order to eliminate any differential understanding of the task. The following sentences were added to the instructions: "Please note that at this imaginary audition you would not be required to recite from memory. You would perform your role by reading from the script."

Table 3.4 provides a comparison between the original actor gist, the original novice gist and the new augmented novice gist conditions. As is seen, the pattern of recall of the two novice groups was remarkably similar; no statistically significant effects emerged. Comparing the augmented gist condition to the actor gist condition, the number of lines recalled of the assigned character was the same, but novices recalled more lines of the other character in the script, $t(26) = 4.59$, $p < .001$, resulting in an overall literal recall advantage for novices, $t(26) = 2.15$, $p < .05$. Therefore, it appears that the recall pattern obtained with novices and actors cannot be attributed to differences in task interpretation. Regardless of instructions, novices showed little tendency to explain what the character was thinking while saying those words.

IMPLICATIONS OF THE ELABORATED RECALL TASK

The elaborations actors generate during script learning may function as powerful retrieval cues by specifying causal relations between the lines they

TABLE 3.4

Mean Number of Lines and Accompanying Thoughts Recalled by Actors and Novices as a Function of Strategy

Category	Actors	Novices	
	Gist	Augmented Gist	Gist
Lines recalled			
Assigned character	15.57	20.43	15.57
Other character	1.93	6.43*	9.29***
Intrusions	0.43	0.64	0.93
Total	17.93	27.50	25.57**
Thoughts recalled			
Explanatory comments	22.5***	9.14	4.86
Nonexplanatory comments	1.71	3.93*	4.86**
Ambiguous	0.57	1.21	0.07
Total	24.79***	14.30	9.79
Grand Total	42.72	41.80	35.43

Note. Independent t-tests:* $p < .05$ between actor and novice gist comparison. **$p < .05$ between actor and augmented gist comparison. ***$p < .05$, between actor gist and both novice gist conditions comparison. From "The Role of Explanations and Plan Recognition in the Learning of Theatrical Scripts," by H. Noice, 1991, *Cognitive Science, 15,* p. 446. Copyright © 1991 by Ablex Publishing Corporation. Reprinted with permission.

are studying and the underlying motivations. For example, one participant reported that while analyzing the line, "It's Monica's scarf," he had the thought, "Austin realizes that Monica may be unfaithful." Thus, it appears an association is formed between the actual line and the interpretive thought. As in a paired association task, the activation of the stimulus (thought) aids the retrieval of the words.

These elaborations also appear to aid actors in their plan recognition process. That is, actors formulate questions about the text and then explain them in terms of the character's overall motivation or intention in the scene. While novices who used a gist strategy also appeared to seek some explanations, they did not ask as many questions, and of those questions they did ask, very few were plan questions. These findings parallel those obtained by Chi, Bassok, Lewis, Reimann, and Glaser (1989), who showed that students who were successful at solving mechanics problems explained and provided justifications for each action. Similarly, Robertson and Swartz (1988) reported that during learning "the proportion of plan questions increases as expertise develops" (p. 51).

NATURE OF A THEATRICAL SCRIPT

These plan questions may be partially prompted by the way most plays are constructed. A careful examination of a theatrical script reveals that it is no more than a blueprint for the finished work. In a novel, the writer can present the attitudes, emotions, and motivations of a character by actually describing his or her unspoken thoughts and feelings. The playwright, however, can only present an objective view (i.e., the words the audience hears and the actions it sees). It is up to the actor to create the character's inner life so that the audience can infer the attitudes, emotions, and motivations from the performance. Only when the audience sees the facial expressions and body language and hears the tone, emphasis, speed, and pauses (in conjunction with the words and actions themselves) can it fully understand the play. It seems probable that the actors' need to make these things clear may make it necessary for them to figure out the character's plan and its various ramifications. And since, as discussed in the Introduction, the essence of acting expertise is to actually do (not pretend to do) what the character would do in that situation, it follows that the actor must implement the character's plans anew at every performance.

Furthermore, as shown, a great many actors actually verbalize the thought the character would be thinking while speaking the line (silent speech). This thought might be complementary, contradictory, or unrelated to the spoken line but would influence channels of communication, such as verbal inflections and facial expressions, necessary to effectively communicate the scripted events to the audience. This elaborative device was used consistently by the majority of the actors in the gist condition (10 out of 14), but rarely by actors in the rote condition (only 3 out of 14 used it with any consistency). Only one novice in the gist condition made extensive use of silent speech. (She also recalled more lines and generated more elaborations than any other novice.) No novice in the rote condition used it.

PROFESSIONAL ACTORS' USE OF PERSPECTIVE

Analysis of the protocols revealed that actors, studying a script as they normally would, elaborate predominantly from the viewpoint of their assigned character. That is, their embellishments are concerned with their own character's wants, needs, and goals and are only concerned with the other characters' motivations in the scene as they pertain to their own. Of course, it would seem natural for any participant to read the scene from the viewpoint of the assigned character, and both novices and actors did so. But analysis of elaborated recall comments showed that actors in the gist condition took on the viewpoint of a character other than their own only 4% of the time, whereas novices did this 20% of the time. That is, novices' comments were made from other characters' perspectives 1 time out of 5, whereas actors' comments of this sort occurred only 1 time in 25.

This perspective taking might help explain actors' reported ease in the learning of long roles. One of the most basic findings in the literature is that if incoming information can be linked to already existing knowledge, this newly acquired information can be recalled more easily than information for which no prior schema exists (e.g., Bransford & Johnson, 1972; Chiesi, Spilich, & Voss, 1979). Thus, perspective functions as a schema and not only aids the encoding, but also the subsequent retrieval of ideas consistent with that particular schema (e.g., Anderson & Pichert, 1978; Dellarosa & Bourne, 1984).

That memory performance is affected by point of view has also been shown by Black et al. (1979). They found that sentences with a single consistent point of view were read faster, comprehended better, and recalled more accurately than sentences in which there was a change in point of view. Lately, there has been a great deal of interest in the relationship between the perspective of the protagonist and the comprehension and memorability of narrative. O'Brien and Albrecht (1992) found that if a sentence containing information on the protagonist's position was inconsistent with information given on his or her position earlier, participants took longer to read the new sentence. However, the effect disappeared when the inconsistent information concerned the actions of a character other than the protagonist. In addition to measuring participants' reading time, O'Brien and Albrecht had their participants recall the passages, but the recall data were not reported. Siegel and Segal (1995) showed that passages in narrative fiction are comprehended better when the author has made clear which character's point of view is operative at the time, and Graesser, Bowers, and Bommareddy (1995) found that readers do track character-specific knowledge.

We believe that the degree to which comprehension and memorability are affected by highly skilled writers' control of perspective warrants further study. Even in third person narration, the nature of the writing itself is responsible for the reader viewing the entire action from the perspective of only one character, shifting perspectives from one character to another, or knowing more than the characters themselves know and hence maintaining a certain psychological distance from the events (Macauley & Lanning, 1964). In fact, because manipulation of viewpoint is one of the writer's main tools for creating emotionally evocative literature, it is almost impossible to write high quality narrative of the type writers refer to as "objective." In this approach, the author only describes observable detail (i.e., what the characters say or do). The characters' (or the author's) thoughts or feelings are never revealed. (Hemingway came very close to bringing off this tour de force in his short story, *The Killers*, 1928, but even here some authorial guidance crept in.)

Plays, however, are necessarily purely objective. The author does not exist for the audience, and each character speaks from his or her own unique perspective. There are, of course, exceptions. Some plays have an on-stage narrator and the events are indeed shown from that narrator's perspective, and some plays appear to be enactments of dreams or mental wanderings. (The original title of *Death of a Salesman* was *Inside Willy's Mind*.) However, most dramas consist of objectively seen events, and our data indicate that actors, but not novices, disregard this objective focus and view all events in terms of how they affect the characters they are playing. This being the case, it seems probable that their perspective-based strategy (and the large number of explanatory elaborations they generate from that perspective) are important contributors to the ease with which actors learn long roles, as reported in the pilot study. But how accurate is the retention of material learned in this manner? And how perishable? These questions are addressed in the next chapter.

4

Cued Recall Task

The results reported in the last chapter, while valuable for specifying the types of embellishments generated, could not accurately determine the extent of verbatim recall or the relative efficiency of rote and gist strategies for at least three reasons: (a) The instructions to write out freely recalled dialogue and accompanying thoughts could possibly bias some participants to report only lines they had extensively elaborated; (b) The reporting of thoughts accompanying one line of dialogue might interfere with the recall of subsequent lines; (c) The task itself of freely recalling dialogue and accompanying thoughts, although necessary for eliciting the participants' elaborations, is quite different from the actor's real-world task (i.e., supplying each line of dialogue as a response to a line of dialogue from another character).

Because, in the elaborated recall task, the primary purpose of a recalled line was to serve as a reference for the accompanying elaborations, how closely that line matched the one in the script was not of interest and credit was given for any utterance containing the idea of the original speech, whether a distant paraphrase or a word-for-word match. Therefore, we designed another task in which participants had to supply each complete speech as a response to the complete speech of the other character in the scene, as in an actual performance (Noice, 1993). Participants were instructed to recall their lines as accurately as possible, but to paraphrase them, if unsure of the exact wording.

They were given a template that only exposed one speech at a time, preventing them from using previous or subsequent lines as prompts, and were allowed as much time as necessary. Furthermore, participants were given this recall task with the cues either in the original order or randomly scrambled. All participants were tested immediately after the elaborated task and, in a surprise recall test, 7 days later. Thus, two other factors were manipulated: order of presentation and time of testing.

It was predicted that a disruption of the temporal ordering of the cues should result in poorer recall for participants using a rote strategy because, when material is learned by rote, the resulting mental representation is likely to be linear instead of hierarchical in structure (Kay & Black, 1986).

It was also predicted that a meaning-based strategy would result in better retention over time.

SCORING

Because, as far as we know, playscripts had never been used as stimulus material, a scoring scheme had to be devised. Accuracy of recall was assessed in two different ways, the first using a strict measure of accuracy (a perfect word-for-word match) and the second using a more lenient one that captured how closely a misremembered line matched the original line. To incorporate both criteria, a special coding system was devised in which each idea unit was scored as follows:

True Verbatim

Only those idea units that were recalled exactly as written in the original playscript were placed in this category.

Almost Verbatim

This was a slightly less strict interpretation of what constitutes verbatim and allowed very minor changes. These included an addition or deletion of a casual locution such as "well" or "hm". Also, interchanging whole forms with contractions was allowed (e. g., "I am so glad you came" instead of "I'm so glad you came.") Either adding or deleting a person's name or interchanging the name with a pronoun was permissible (e. g., "I asked Storey to bring you to my house" instead of "I asked him to bring you to my house.")

The final rule in this category concerned the subordinate conjunction "that" when used to introduce a subordinate clause. It was acceptable to either omit or add it. For example: "It's comforting to know that even a scientific genius is not immune" instead of "It's comforting to know even a scientific genius is not immune" was permissible. Two of these minor changes were allowed in a single idea unit. However, if the changes under these rules constituted 50% or more of the idea unit, that unit then could not be considered accurately recalled and had to be scored as a paraphrase.

Deviation Verbatim

Because this was a slightly more lenient measure, only a single change per idea unit was allowed. However, it was permissible to combine it with a single instance of the "almost verbatim" category. These are some examples of some of the permissible changes:

- One-word additions or deletions that didn't result in a change of meaning such as "It must have taken *her* a long time" instead of "It must have taken a long time."
- The substitution of a single word in the same grammatical class, provided that the meaning of the idea unit was preserved. For example, "Didn't you *drive* her home?" instead of "Didn't you *take* her home?"
- The substitution of a verb for a verb–noun phrase such as, "You *dined* here with her" instead of "You *had dinner* here with her."
- Any form of the same verb was permissible, including positive–negative inversion and emphatic form. For example, "Are you *planning to marry* Storey?" instead of "Are you *planning on marrying* Storey?"
- It was also permissible to omit redundant terminal words, such as "didn't you" or "wouldn't it." For example, "You dined here with her?" instead of "You dined here with her, didn't you?"

The aim of this coding scheme was to differentiate verbatim recall from recall that was so close to verbatim it could not properly be categorized as a mere paraphrase. All the rules were generated by analyzing commonalities during the first 10 scoring sessions. Only after a complete scoring scheme had been developed were independent raters trained.

Nearly Verbatim

To allow assessment of accuracy within specifically defined limits, we created this additional measure in which true verbatim, almost verbatim, and deviation verbatim were collapsed into a single measure. It should be pointed out that these rules were so strict that even certain two-word changes in long complex sentences would prevent the utterances from being designated as *nearly verbatim*.

Paraphrases

Any idea units that contained changes other than the minor exceptions mentioned were scored as paraphrases. These included meaning-preserving summaries of two or more statements.

Guesses and Intrusions

Incorrect utterances that appeared to have been derived from the context were classified as *contextual guesses*. Any actual lines recalled correctly but to the wrong cue were categorized as *incorrect-order intrusions*. (See Table 4.1 for the entire scoring scheme.)

TABLE 4.1

Scoring Scheme for Assessing Accuracy of Recall

Category	Definition
1. True verbatim	Absolute word-for-word recall of the text
2. Almost verbatim	Minor changes are permitted. For example:
	1. Omission or addition of casual locutions (e. g., "She probably ran back to tell Storey something" instead of, "Well, she probably ran back to tell Storey something").
	2. Interchanging of whole forms with contractions (e. g., "I'm so glad you came" instead of "I am so glad you came").
	3. Addition or omission of a person's name in an address (e. g., "It would be nice for you, Austin because you understand all about those things" versus "It would be nice for you because you understand all about those things").
3. Deviation verbatim	Allows any one of the following deviations providing the meaning of the idea unit remains intact:
	1. One-word additions that don't result in a change of meaning (e. g., "It must have taken a long time" versus "It must have taken her a long time").
	2. Switching of two words in the same phrase (e. g., "You dined with her here?" versus "You dined here with her?").
	3. Switching a word for one in the same grammatical class (e. g., "Maybe he doesn't know everything" instead of "Perhaps he doesn't know everything").
	4. Addition of the conjunctions *but* and *and* (e. g., "I was here promptly at eleven. Storey hadn't even begun to dress" versus "I was here promptly at eleven and Storey hadn't even begun to dress").

Note. Items with changes other than the above were considered as "not recalled" and were scored as paraphrases or intrusions. From "Effects of Strategy on the Verbatim Retention of Theatrical Scripts," by H. Noice, 1993, *Applied Cognitive Psychology, 7*, pp. 80–83. Copyright © 1993 by John Wiley. Adapted with permission.

Reliability of Scoring

The cued recall protocols in both conditions (immediate and delayed) were scored by one judge. After three training sessions with materials from another playscript, two independent raters scored a random subset of 37 recall protocols (one scored 19 protocols and one scored 18 others). Agreements between the main judge and the independent raters ranged from 95% (for contextual guesses) to 99% (for verbatim). Any disputed cases were resolved by an additional independent rater.

RECALL PERFORMANCE

True Verbatim Recall

Values of $p < .05$ were considered significant for all analyses. To address word-for-word accuracy, the mean percentages of idea units recalled with absolute fidelity were calculated. Table 4.2 summarizes the data, showing scores in both immediate and delayed testing.

The data were examined using a mixed analysis of variance with three between-subjects factors: expertise (actors vs. students), strategy (rote vs. gist), and order (cues in normal vs. scrambled order), and one within-subjects factor: time of testing (immediate vs. delay). The most important finding was that in every instance, participants in the gist condition far outperformed participants in the rote condition, $F(1, 48) = 25.30, MSe = 402.87$. These results, however, need to be qualified by a significant interaction between expertise and strategy, $F(1, 48) = 4.92, MSe = 402.87$. An analysis of simple effects revealed that although students' recall was depressed significantly under rote instructions, $F(1, 48) = 26.27, MSe =$

TABLE 4.2

Mean Percentage of Idea Units Scored as True Verbatim as a Function of Group, Strategy, Order, and Time of Testing

	Actors				Students			
	Rote		Gist		Rote		Gist	
	Regular	Scrambled	Regular	Scrambled	Regular	Scrambled	Regular	Scrambled
Immediate								
M	14.30	19.97	32.74	27.83	6.20	5.86	39.57	38.67
SD	7.8	14.45	21.11	18.75	3.52	5.18	27.22	25.48
Delay								
M	7.10	11.01	19.01	15.46	3.80	5.16	26.59	25.86
SD	6.53	5.62	12.66	15.46	3.50	5.21	12.52	18.51

Note. From "Effects of Strategy on the Verbatim Retention of Theatrical Scripts," by H. Noice, 1993, Applied Cognitive Psychology, 7, p. 77. Copyright © 1993 by John Wiley. Adapted with permission.

TABLE 4.3
Mean Percentage of Idea Units Scored as Nearly Verbatim, True Verbatim or Paraphrase as a Function of Expertise, Strategy and Time of Testing

	Immediate Test			
	Actors		Novices	
	Rote	Gist	Rote	Gist
Nearly verbatim	23.8	41.7	10.3	51.3
True verbatim	(17.1)	(30.3)	(6.0)	(39.1)
Paraphrase	11.5	17.2	8.7	16.2
Total recall	35.3	58.9	19.0	67.5
	Delayed Test			
	Actors		Novices	
	Rote	Gist	Rote	Gist
Nearly verbatim	12.5	24.0	16.3	40.3
True verbatim	(9.1)	(17.2)	(4.3)	(26.2)
Paraphrase	10.0	16.3	7.1	17.1
Total recall	22.5	40.3	13.2	53.5

Note. From "Effects of Strategy on the Verbatim Retention of Theatrical Scripts," by H. Noice, 1993, Applied Cognitive Psychology, 7, p. 78. Copyright © 1993 by John Wiley. Adapted with permission.

402.87, this decrement was only marginally significant for actors, $F(1, 48 = 3.95, p = .05, MSe = 402.87$. One way to interpret this interaction is that actors might have been more capable of defeating the constraints of a rote strategy.

Delayed testing resulted in an overall decrease in recall scores, $F(1, 48) = 55.69$, $MSe = 40.10$, and it interacted with strategy, $F(1, 48) = 11.40$, $MSe = 40.10$. This interaction reflected the fact that although forgetting occurred for material studied by rote, $F(1, 48) = 8.35$, $MSe = 40.10$, significantly more material was forgotten that had been studied by gist, $F(1, 48) = 58.75$, $MSe = 40.10$. However, these results could be due to floor effects because on the immediate test, participants in the rote condition remembered only about 12% of the material with complete word-for-word fidelity; this decreased to less than 7% one week later. The important finding is that about 22% of the material studied by gist was still remembered with complete word-for-word accuracy even in surprise delayed testing. Finally, there was no significant main effect of order, nor did order interact with any of the other factors. Consequently, the analyses that follow are collapsed over the order variable.

Overall Recall

Of additional interest was how much of the text could be remembered when deviations from the original wordings were allowed. Therefore, two additional dependent measures were used: *nearly verbatim* (a combination of true verbatim, almost verbatim, and deviation verbatim), and *total recall* (a combination of nearly verbatim and paraphrases). These means are presented in Table 4.3.

Nearly Verbatim Recall

A second analysis of variance was carried out for nearly verbatim recall scores only. Again, most interesting for present purposes was the obvious superiority of a gist strategy compared to a rote strategy, $F(1, 52) = 37.10$, $MSe = 478.22$. More of the text was recalled verbatim by participants who had been instructed to study it by attending to the assigned character rather than by repeating the individual speeches. However, apparently expertise affords the advantage of being able to compensate for an inferior strategy, as shown by a significant interaction of expertise and strategy, $F(1, 52) = 6.46, MSe = 478.22$. That is, actors performed significantly better under the strict conditions imposed by a rote strategy than did students. An analysis of simple main effects showed that use of a rote strategy resulted in a greater deficit in students' recall, $F(1, 52) = 37.30, MSe = 478.22$, than in actors' recall, $F(1, 52) = 6.30, MSe = 478.22$.

Retention after 7 days was superior for participants using a gist strategy, $F(1,52 = 12.30, MSe = 41.27$. Although delayed testing revealed considerable forgetting for participants in all experimental conditions, $F(1, 52) = 98.33, MSe = 41.27$, more of the material learned with a gist strategy was forgotten compared to material learned by rote, $F(1, 52) = 90.08, MSe = 41.27$, possibly due to floor effects. The important finding is that after a 1-week delay, participants in the gist condition still remembered 32% of the playscript verbatim or nearly verbatim. However, the recall level one week later showed a greater decrease on the part of actors, $F(1, 52) = 71.84$, $MSe = 41.27$, than students, $F(1, 52) = 30.77, MSe = 41.27$. Since all actors were engaged in studying other roles at the time, interference effects might possibly account for this disparate decrease.

Paraphrases

Because the gist instructions emphasized thinking about the character, it might seem likely that participants would have attended more to the meaning of the character's speeches than to the exact words and would have shown a tendency to paraphrase. However, as shown in Table 4.3, the reverse was true: Participants paraphrased considerably fewer lines than they recalled verbatim. In general, participants in both groups did very little paraphrasing (M = 16.7% in the gist condition and M = 10.1% in the rote condition), indicating that even when participants are encouraged to attend to the meaning of the text, they appear to be closely attending to its exact words as well.

To assess overall recall, paraphrases were added to nearly verbatim (these totals are also given in Table 4.3) and subjected to an analysis of variance. In general, the obtained pattern of results was very similar to that of the analysis that used nearly verbatim as the dependent measure. As in the previous analysis, a significant interaction between group and strategy emerged, $F(1, 52) = 7.69$, $MSe = 510.85$, showing that, whereas actors and students performed equally well in the gist condition, actors outperformed students under the stringent rules imposed by a rote condition, $F(1, 52) = 4.48$, $MSe = 510.85$. Furthermore, participants in the gist condition remembered significantly more lines of the playscript than did participants in the rote condition, $F(1, 52) = 58.04$, $MSe = 510.85$, and again there was evidence of considerable forgetting in that 1-week interval, $F(1, 52) = 89.59$, $MSe = 51.05$.

Lines that were recalled correctly but to the wrong cue were not counted in the overall recall scores. However, these importations occurred infrequently.

Guessing

Material that had not occurred in the text but that may have been derived from context appeared to play a very minor role. On the immediate test, participants in the gist condition had (on the average) about 2 guesses; this increased to 3.8 guessses 1 week later. Participants in the rote condition maintained about the same guess rate during both times of testing, 3 guesses in the immediate condition and 3.6 guesses in the delayed condition. To assess the effect of expertise and strategy on guessing, an additional analysis of variance was carried out. The only reliable effect was that of time of testing, $F(1, 52) = 11.51$ and $MSe = 3.7$, indicating that participants engaged in more contextual guessing 1 week after testing than in immediate testing.

DISCUSSION

This task was designed to investigate whether a gist strategy is superior to a rote one in terms of verbatim retention and, if so, whether this superiority would hold up regardless of the participants' experience in the learning of theatrical scripts. The findings revealed that participants using a gist strategy not only far outperformed participants using a rote strategy, but that this strategy advantage was particularly true for students. That is, these students recalled five times as much material (scored as nearly verbatim) as those who had tried to memorize the same material in a rote fashion. Although this pattern was also true for actors, the disparity was not as great.

The comparatively high degree of verbatim recall obtained with a meaning-based strategy may have been partially due to the nature of the material. The reader of a playscript must imagine not only the tone of voice and the gestures but also the moods and motivations of the characters. For instance, in a novel the author might write, "She resented his overbearing ways but held her tongue and simply said, 'Good night'." In a play, the man would have a piece of a dialogue that suggested his overbearing ways and the woman's dialogue would only consist of the words "Good night." Her attitude (based on the man's overbearing remark) would have to be imagined by the reader, involving extensive embellishment of the actual text.

Anderson and Reder (1979) argued that such elaborations provide redundancy, increasing the number of retrieval cues. In addition to redundancy, these elaborations increase task complexity, another factor shown to increase memorability of text. McDaniel (1981) showed that when sentences are presented in embedded form, participants exhibit better memory for the exact wording. His explanation was that embedded sentences were more difficult to process than sentences in standard form and therefore elicited more elaborations. Relating this to our material, the dialogue, devoid of descriptions of how the character felt, may have induced the reader to seek clues to its meaning by focusing on the exact words, rendering them and their arrangement distinctive and memorable. The power of distinctiveness has been demonstrated by Mantyla (1986). His participants were shown 504 words on three consecutive days with the instructions to generate a unique, distinctive description for each consisting of either one or three words. On the third day, participants were presented with their own generated descriptions and instructed to recall the corresponding words. When given their three-word descriptions, they recalled more than 90% of the target words.

Another explanation for our results might be that actively understanding material involves mental effort and the more effort exerted during encoding of an item, the better the retention of that item. Several studies have confirmed a relationship between effort and memory (e.g., Jacoby, Craik, & Begg, 1979; O'Brien & Myers, 1985; Tyler, Hertel, McCallum, & Ellis, 1979). For example, O'Brien and Myers (1985) manipulated encoding difficulty by inserting a target word that was either predictable or unpredictable from the context. This manipulation led to an increase in reading time for the text preceding the target word and to an improvement in recall. The researchers suggested that forcing participants to go back and reprocess portions of a text increased the effort participants had to expend on the task and, as a consequence, facilitated memory for that portion of the text. Although mental effort was not specifically manipulated in our experiment, one could argue that more effort was required of the participants who were told to think about a character in the text than participants who were told to keep repeating it. That this effort was indeed made was shown in the elaborated recall task, described in chapter 3, in which participants in the gist condition generated about 8 times as many explanatory elaborations as those in the rote condition.

The superior results of gist over rote for students are particularly interesting because this disparity was not as strong for actors. Apparently this was due to the actors' ability to defeat the constraints of the rote strategy. In addition to their written strategy statements (described in the next chapter), many participants initiated posttest discussions. These revealed that the actors hated the experimental procedure in the rote condition. They expressed great frustration over not being allowed to go back and look over the earlier material. Some actors said that, although they really tried to memorize by sheer rote, they nevertheless found themselves relating the meaning of the old information to the new as they were repeating it. They further commented that they could not help thinking of possible motives or intentions. On the other hand, students in the rote condition reported no such behavior. These informal posttest statements, although only anecdotal, are nevertheless interesting inasmuch as actor after actor in the rote condition insisted on telling the experimenter of the extreme frustration experienced.

In keeping with previous work (e. g., Craik & Watkins, 1973; Rundus, 1977), our results suggest that repetition of text does not necessarily transfer it to long-term memory even when the participant's intention was to memorize it and when each sentence was repeated about 10 times. On the other hand, a learning strategy based on elaborating the material did lead to significant verbatim retention. Thus, these results provide evidence that an elaborative strategy is an effective one even for tasks requiring word-for-word retention of complex material.

At first glance, the results of this experiment appear to conflict with those obtained by Intons-Peterson and Smyth (1987) showing excellent recall for student actors in the rote condition. However, in that study, the only constraint placed on rote participants was that they could not read the entire paragraph before starting to memorize. Those participants were not constrained from thinking about the meaning of each sentence and the relation it bore to the preceding sentence. This ability to elaborate as they studied might well explain their pattern of recall. In our experiment the rote condition constraints were designed to minimize the possibility that in the course of studying the text, a gist strategy would inadvertently be introduced. We feel that a great deal of confusion exists because of the various ways in which the term rote is used. When many people refer to learning something by rote, it is probable that they really mean they learn it by first understanding it, then repeating it. The procedure here was designed to investigate the results of rote learning in the strict definition of the term (by repetition alone).

It might be argued that the actors' performance in the present experiment was due to their experience in studying material presented in playscript format. However, the student group that used a gist strategy remembered about 40% of a highly complex text verbatim. Yet, these students had no background in the performance or reading of playscripts. Therefore, previous exposure to the format of complex material does not appear to influence the memory process as much as does the strategy of the learner.

A question might be asked regarding the excellent recall performance of students in the gist condition. Because actors have extensive experience in the memorization of dialogue, why did they not outperform students? One reason might be simply that college students are also fairly experienced learners. Another reason might be that actors in the gist condition spent more of their study time explaining the text. The elaborated recall task showed that they generated 2 ½ times as many explanatory elaborations as students in the same condition. That this generating of elaborations by questioning the text is indeed time-consuming has been demonstrated by Frase (1975). He showed that students who had been told to construct questions of a text took twice as much time as students who merely had to study the same text.

The results of this research may be viewed in the context of work conducted by Einstein and Hunt (1980) and Hunt and Einstein (1981) who suggested that optimal retention of material occurs when participants use both relational and individual-item processing. Relational processing refers to the adding of information not explicitly mentioned in the text in order to establish coherence; individual-item processing refers to attending closely to each individual word. In one of the studies (Einstein & Hunt, 1980, Experiment 2), structure of the stimulus material was manipulated to encourage participants to use either one or both encoding processes. In our study, the constraints under which rote subjects operated more or less excluded relational processing and required participants to primarily use individual-item processing, resulting in the extremely poor recall performance.

Conversely, the participants in the gist condition were specifically instructed to think about the character they were to portray, thus encouraging these participants to determine the meaning of their character's actions. However, the meaning in a playscript is not as explicit as in other forms of prose and must be teased out by the reader. The only way to tease out this meaning is by establishing coherence. This requires attending to the individual words and understanding why the character used those particular words.

Thus the nature of a playscript seems to require both relational and individual-item processing in order to be made coherent. Perhaps the proper question to ask is not whether a rote or a gist strategy is better suited for memorizing a passage, but what combination of attending to both the meaning of the passage and the specific words used to express that meaning yields the best results.

It appears that much of the controversy regarding rote and gist learning stems from the fact that relatively few experiments have used conditions restricting learning to "rote" as that term is almost invariably defined in dictionaries and cognitive textbooks (i.e., with little or no attending to meaning).

CONCLUSION

This study set out to compare the effects of rote versus gist learning for both professional actors and undergraduate students. The results suggest that rote memorization is a very inefficient strategy for both groups, even for material that must be learned verbatim.

Following this cued recall task, we had participants perform two additional tasks. The first was summarization, a paradigm frequently used to infer the nature of mental representations. The second consisted of the generation of posttest statements that offered further insights into the strategies of actors and students when studying the same script. The results of those investigations are reported in the next chapter.

5

The Summarization Task and Posttest Statements of Strategy

It seems probable that a professional actor who elaborates and explains the text by inferring the characters' intersecting plans generates a representation of the text that is qualitatively different from that of a novice who has no experience in role preparation. Therefore, differences should be observed in the types of statements that participants in either condition include in their summaries. (Qualitative differences in the representations of expert and novice physicists as revealed by their summaries were reported by Chi et al., 1982). There is also an abundance of evidence to show that within a narrative, goal statements have a high probability of being included in a summary, have a high degree of memorability, and are usually rated as most important (e.g., Abbott, Black, & Smith, 1985; Black & Bower, 1980; Bower, 1982; Chiesi et al., 1979; Lichtenstein & Brewer, 1989; Owens et al., 1979; Trabasso & van den Broek, 1985; van den Broek, 1988; van den Broek & Trabasso, 1986). Because actors approach the task of understanding a script by trying to identify the plans their assigned characters are pursuing vis-à-vis the other characters, some of the statements included in the actors' summaries should concern the emotional interactions that constitute the implementation of those plans. And, because novices generated few goal-directed elaborations during script study, it would be surprising if they did so during summarization.

Furthermore, if the differences between novices and actors in their generation of summary statements were to parallel the differences found in their retrospective protocols, actors would be expected to summarize actions from the perspectives of the characters in the script, whereas novices should appear to stand outside the story and summarize it objectively.

SCORING PROCEDURES

Because examining each utterance as a whole best reveals the participant's viewpoint, we adopted the independent clause as the unit of analysis. The following scoring procedure was created: Each main verb of the clause was categorized as either an action verb (transitive or intransitive) or a nonaction verb (copulative). Following this grammatical analysis, content analysis tried to discern if the meaning of the clause involved an emotional interaction between two characters, dispositional properties of one or more of the characters, or physical or mental activity. Raters followed a strict series of rules:

1. Does the main verb indicate an emotional or internal state (e.g., loves, fears, confesses, doubts, reassures, etc)? If so, look at the grammatical subject and the direct or indirect object to see if the interaction is explicitly stated (e.g., "Kendall reassures Austin"). If the object is not directly stated, is it unequivocally implied? (e.g., "He confesses his fears" [to her]). If so, list the clause as emotional interaction (transitive or intransitive).

2. If the presence of an internal state cannot be determined by that analysis, then the entire predicate must be considered (e.g., "Through the sharing of their feelings a bond is created"). This particular example would be listed as an *interactive state of being*.

3. Physical activities and speech acts are generally easily determined by the use of verbs such as meet, enter, talk, discuss, etc. In addition to categorizing these interactions, the raters designated who performed it ("same" for assigned character, "different" for the other character in the scene, "both" for Austin and Kendall together, and "other" for characters referred to but not present).

After performing the grammatical and content analysis, the scorer posed two questions of the summaries. First, was there an indication of temporal ordering? Because a very brief summary obviously does not allow for a complete chronological organization, only the first sentence was examined. If it was a restatement of the opening stage directions and/or of the first line of the script, it would be an indication of temporal ordering. That is, it would indicate that the participants' mental representation began with the first information in the script. Second, did a statement in the summary indicate the participant had inferred the goal or resolution of the scene that had not been explicitly stated in the text? (We asked a well-known director/writer to summarize the scene and explicitly state the resolution that the author had implied. In his view, this implied resolution was that the two characters were warming toward each other, J. W. Kirk, personal communication, September 3, 1987).

Reliability of Scoring

All of the summaries were scored by the main rater (the experimenter). A randomly selected subset of 25 protocols was scored blindly by an independent rater. Interrater reliability was 1.00 for all categories except emotional interactions versus activities which was .94. Finally, these few disagreements were resolved by an additional independent rater.

RESULTS AND DISCUSSION

Types of Clauses

The total number of independent clauses was calculated for each of the following categories: emotional interactions, speech acts/physical activities, unelaborated states of being, and dispositional properties. Mean percentages for each category were calculated. These data, and the results of the independent-measures t-tests, are shown in Table 5.1.

As predicted, actors in the gist condition produced a greater percentage of sentences that described emotional interactions as compared to novices, $t(54) = 2.01, p < .05$. Also, they produced a lower percentage of verbal utterances concerned with mental or physical activities compared to any other experimental condition, $t(26) = -2.45, p < .05$. This appeared to indicate that actors in the gist condition used a hierarchical approach, considering physical and speech acts as less important for their purposes than emotional interactions. Participants in all other conditions

TABLE 5.1

Mean Percentage of Summary Statements by Category Type as a Function of Group and Strategy

	Actors		Novices	
	Rote	Gist	Rote	Gist
Interactions	34.9	55.1	30.0	37.5
Mental or physical activities	58.7	36.7	50.0	47.9
Dispositional properties	.0	.0	4.0	.0
Unelaborated state	6.4	8.2	16.0	14.6
Total	100.0	100.0	100.0	100.0

Note. From "The Role of Explanations and Plan Recognition in the Learning of Theatrical Scripts," by H. Noice, 1991, Cognitive Science, 15, p. 447. Copyright © 1991 by Ablex Publishing Corporation. Reprinted with permission.

included fewer psychological interactions and more mental or physical activities when summarizing the scene. In general, participants showed very little tendency to summarize the playscript in terms of dispositional properties.

Furthermore, in the gist condition actors tended to couch their sentences in an active form (e.g., "Kendall reassures him that his doubts are unfounded") rather than the more static form preferred by novices (e.g., "Kendall is in love with Storey"). This finding suggests that actors are more likely to encode a playscript as an unfolding process than as a fixed entity.

Another question was whether novices were more prone to use copulative (linking) verbs than actors. Because these verbs, by definition, denote a state of being, this would be evidence for a reporting style rather than an interpretive one. Summed across strategy, novices generated a greater percentage of summary sentences using linking verbs than actors did (35.6% vs. 20.7%). Moreover, novices who had studied the text using a rote strategy were the most likely to summarize using linking verbs (42%). For each participant, difference scores between the number of sentences using linking verbs and transitive or intransitive verbs were computed. An independent-groups t-test confirmed that actors and novices differed significantly in the types of verb forms they used, $t(54) = 2.5, p < .05$. Finally, even when employing copulative verbs, actors tended to be more elaborative than static. For example, one actor wrote, "Mrs. Frayne is alternately playful and comforting to him," whereas a novice wrote, "It appears that Kendall is in love with Storey." An examination of all statements using copulative verbs showed that novices were twice as likely as actors to summarize the scene in terms of static state descriptions (15.3% for novices vs. 7.3% for actors). Thus, novices were far more prone than actors to make summary statements like, "This is a scene about a man and a woman."

USE OF PERSPECTIVE

From a statement such as, "Kendall is reassuring the upset Austin," one immediately infers that this reassurance constitutes Kendall's goal or intention in this emotional interaction. Conversely, statements such as, "They're in Story's apartment," or "They talk about Monica," lack intentionality and, as a result, constitute the other side of this dichotomy. Therefore all statements were classified as simply presenting information or conveying how the assigned character actively affected the other character. These results are shown in Table 5.2.

We found that actors in the gist condition generated more than twice as many emotional interaction summary statements from the viewpoint of their assigned character as from the viewpoint of the other character (28.6 % vs. 10.2 %). On the other hand, participants in all other conditions were equally likely to write statements concerning these emotional interactions from either the perspective of their assigned character or from the perspective of the other

TABLE 5.2
Mean Percentage of Summary Statements Made from Perspective of Assigned Character Versus Other Character by Activity Type

	Emotional Interactions		Other Activities	
	Assigned	Other	Assigned	Other
Actors				
Rote	12.7	11.1	20.6	12.7
Gist	28.6	12.2	16.3	4.0
Novices				
Rote	14.0	12.0	24.0	6.0
Gist	8.3	8.3	14.6	4.2

Note. From "The Role of Explanations and Plan Recognition in the Learning of Theatrical Scripts," by H. Noice, 1991, *Cognitive Science, 15,* p. 449. Copyright © 1991 by Ablex Publishing Corporation. Reprinted with permission.

character. For each participant, difference scores between the number of emotional interactions from the viewpoint of the assigned character as opposed to the other character in the script were computed. An independent-groups t-test confirmed that actors and novices differed significantly in terms of how likely they were to adopt the perspective of the assigned character, $t(26) = 2.09, p < .05$.

INFERRED RESOLUTION AND TEMPORAL ORDERING

Eight out of 14 actors in the gist condition mentioned the probable resolution as part of their summaries, whereas only 4 out of 14 of actors in the rote condition did. For the novices, 4 out of 14 in the gist condition included the resolution, but none in the rote condition did. A chi-square analysis showed a significant relationship between expertise and the inclusion of the inferred resolution, $X^2(1, N = 56) = 5.6, p < .05$.

Of additional interest was whether participants tended to adhere to the temporal ordering of the text when summarizing the scene. An order different from the original input could imply that hierarchical (goal-directed) reorganization had taken place. It was found that, in the gist condition, only 21% of the actors adhered to the temporal ordering compared to 43% of the novices. In the rote condition both groups scored 57% along this dimension. However, a chi-square analysis applied to the data did not quite reach significance, $X^2(1, N = 56) = 3.54, p > .05$.

INFERRING THE STRUCTURE OF THE MENTAL REPRESENTATION

The results of the summarization task indicated that professional actors and novices had widely differing mental representations, and that these differences appeared to mirror the differences found in the elaborated recall protocols of both groups. Although all summaries included both text events and elaborations, actors in the gist condition included far more elaborations, particularly concerning the emotional interactions of the characters. Compared to participants in the other experimental conditions, these actors generated the greatest percentage of statements concerning how characters in the play affected each other emotionally and the smallest percentage of statements concerning physical or mental actions.

Furthermore, novices summarized the scene statically (e.g., "There were two people in this scene") more than twice as often as actors, providing additional evidence that participants' summaries reflected their encoding processes. That is, actors tried to explain the scene by inferring the characters' goals from the dialogue. A plausible hypothesis is that the actors' goal-type statements are inserted in a plan hierarchy at a level higher than that of actions, and when asked to generate a summary, participants include information they judge to be most important. Furthermore, the actors' greater tendency to ignore the temporal ordering of the script was taken as an additional indication that they used high-level knowledge structures (plans) during understanding.

Finally, the tendency of actors in the gist condition to engage in deep processing of the text (including inference making) was demonstrated by the fact that in the gist condition, twice as many actors included the implied resolution in their summaries as did novices. However, learning by sheer repetition does not appear to induce the generation of inferences, as shown by the fact that in the rote condition none of the novices and only 29% of the actors alluded to the resolution of the scene.

Overall, these results are in line with previous research on text comprehension, which has shown that participants who understand a narrative as a plan to reach a goal select goal statements for inclusion in a summary (e.g., Abbott & Black, 1986; Fletcher, 1984; Kay & Black, 1986; Kintsch, 1977; Kintsch & van Dijk, 1975; Rumelhart, 1975; Trabasso & van den Broek, 1985; van den Broek & Trabasso, 1986).

ANALYSIS OF POSTTEST STATEMENTS OF STRATEGY

The posttest strategy statements were given to an independent rater who had no knowledge of the purpose of the experiment. The rater was told to analyze the statements for commonalities, title those commonalities, and list those statements that fell in each category. The rater was blind with respect to condition as well as overall design, to insure against experimenter bias in the assigning of statements to categories. Clear differences emerged in terms of the type of strategy participants reported using during the 20-minute study session. Thirteen out of 14 actors in the gist condition stressed active understanding of the assigned characters' motivations and their relationships to the other characters in the play. Among the students, there was little unanimity. The most frequently mentioned strategies were "read for content" (6 participants) and "visualize the scene" (6 participants). Less frequently mentioned were "test own recall of lines" (4 participants) and "associate lines with one another" (2 participants).

These strategy descriptions showed that almost all the actors were concerned with deep understanding of the character's goals and motivations. Only 1 out of the 14 even mentioned eventually having to memorize the lines, and then only as a secondary issue. Students reported using a wide variety of devices, such as visualizations and repeated readings. Thus, both groups appeared to use versions of gist strategies most suited to their needs. The actors' statements indicated great depth of processing; they consistently reported probing the characters' underlying thought processes. On the other hand, the students reported using many of the strategies frequently used to learn assigned text material. Thus the students and the actors both used forms of gist strategy that gave them the results they desired, and with both groups, these results were far superior to those obtained by using a rote strategy. It might be objected that actors' strategy statements possibly reflected the norms of their profession rather than the actual procedure they used. However, in this particular experiment, the strategy statements simply added converging evidence to what the elaborated recall task had already demonstrated.

CONCLUSION

The summaries generated by actors and students showed clear differences between their mental representations, with the actors demonstrating a far greater tendency to organize text hierarchically and to adopt the assigned characters' perspectives. The posttest statements of strategy reinforced our conclusions regarding these differences, as revealed both by the summaries reported in this chapter and by the actors' and students' protocols, described in chapter 3.

While the research described in this and the two previous chapters provided an overall view of actors' mental representations of their roles, it did not entail an in-depth analysis of how actors understand the unstated implications of each portion of the text. This was provided later by a lengthy think-aloud protocol described in the next chapter.

6

A Professional Actor Prepares a Role: A Think-Aloud Protocol

Data derived from retrospective protocols have two drawbacks: Hindsight rationalizations may have occurred, and a complete picture of the process under investigation is not available because some forgetting is bound to have taken place (cf., Nisbett & Wilson, 1977). Therefore, having sketched out a broad picture of dozens of actors' mental processes during script study with retrospective protocols, we decided to collect a detailed think-aloud protocol from a single actor. He dictated every thought, as it occurred, while he worked his way from the first line of dialogue to the last. This approach has been shown to be sensitive to the strategic elements of comprehension (Ericsson, 1988; Ericsson & Simon, 1984), and it is strategic elements that this study specifically examines.

The protocol was generated by an experienced male actor (T. D.) with both formal training (an MFA degree from a major university) and extensive professional experience. The playscript was the same as that used by Noice (1991), a five-page scene for two characters from the play *The Second Man* by S. N. Behrman (1952).

Heretofore, think-aloud protocols have been used to capture the mental processes involved in two types of tasks: those with which the participant has no prior experience and therefore no specific procedural knowledge; and those to which the participant can apply his or her existing procedural knowledge, even though the exemplar itself is new. Our protocol is of the latter type. It was generated in a single session of approximately 35 minutes.

After being told that the purpose of this experiment was to make a record of the thoughts that go through a professional actor's mind in the course of studying a script, the participant was questioned as to his usual procedure in preparing a role. He stated that he would first read through the script quickly, then go back to the beginning and start his preparation. He was given the script, told he would be preparing the role of Austin, and asked to read the scene exactly as he would on his first read-through. This took approximately 5 minutes.

In most problem-solving protocols, the participant is first presented with a description of the entire problem. Only after reading or hearing the description does the participant start the think-aloud procedure. Because this task consisted of learning a scene, the first read-through was in actuality the statement of the problem. That is, the task was to analyze the script for the purpose of learning it; therefore, the first reading acquainted the participant with the problem he had to solve and thus served the same purpose as the description of the Tower of Hanoi problem in the Anzai and Simon (1979) study. This procedure mirrors what many actors have reported as one they usually use (Noice, 1991).

The participant was given a small tape recorder and was instructed to verbalize his thoughts as they came to him while he worked on the script. He was specifically told not to censor anything that he considered extraneous or unsuitable, but simply to leave the microphone on as he followed his usual procedure, thinking aloud as he went along. To avoid reactivity, the experimenter left the room and did not return until the participant had completed the task.

The think-aloud comments were then transcribed. (The punctuation was derived from T. D.'s speech pattern; it reflects pauses, hesitations, parenthetical comments, full stops, etc.) The entire protocol, broken down into numbered utterances (referred to as protocol statements), is found in Appendix B. The classification of the components of this protocol is shown in Table 6.1.

TABLE 6.1

Organization of T. D.'s Transcribed Think-Aloud Protocol

Opening comments	
Metastatements	1
Main body	
Organizing statements	9
Metastatements	14
PSUs	65
Extraneous comments	4
Closing comments	
Metastatements	4
Extraneous comments	1
Combined total	96

Note. From "An Example of Role Preparation by a Professional Actor: A Think-Aloud Protocol," by H. Noice and T. Noice, 1994, *Discourse Processes, 18,* p. 349. Copyright © 1994 by Ablex Publishing Corporation. Reprinted with permission.

As we see, the protocol consisted of three sections: (a) opening comments in which T. D. introduced his general approach to any script, (b) the main body in which T. D. went through this particular script, digging out what he regarded as the important information, and interpreting, analyzing, and elaborating on it, and (c) closing comments, once again about the participant's general working procedure.

From repeated readings of the protocol, it became obvious that T. D. had regarded his task as a problem-solving one. He had examined the written material and from it derived the character's intentions and motivations and the ways in which he would move, talk, and interact with the other character in the script. Therefore, it was decided that the most applicable unit of analysis (the one that would best capture the participant's mental processes) would be what we termed *problem-solving units* (PSUs). Most PSUs consisted of one to four phrases or sentences. However, one exceptionally long unit contained 17 phrases or sentences. Nevertheless, since these concerned a single problem, they were scored as a single problem-solving unit.

In addition to these PSUs, the main body of the protocol contained 12 metastatements about the participant's general procedure (similar to those found in his opening and closing comments). These metastatements, consisting of one or more sentences, concerned either a procedure the participant generally followed or, specifically, the process by which the participant would commit material to memory (e.g., "And the more clues you have to each one, the more context you have, the faster you memorize it and the more natural it comes out," protocol statement # 74).

The main body also contained nine organizing statements. These organizing statements were not concerned with deriving information from the text; they simply divided it into sections which T. D. called beats. For example, he isolated one beat with the statement, "Starting with him noticing Monica's colored scarf and going on, scanning here, to the end of his line, 'Storey hadn't even begun to dress'" (protocol statement # 35).

Except for these metastatements and organizing statements, all utterances in the protocol were of the type referred to as problem-solving units. In these 65 PSUs, the actor used information in the script to infer the characters' intentions, motivations, mental/emotional states and/or performance characteristics. Because these PSUs offer insight into the actor's mental processes during role preparation, they are analyzed in detail in the next section of this chapter. When appropriate, descriptive statistics are supplied to give some indication of the frequency with which certain strategies were employed and thus their apparent importance. In addition to these categories, the participant made occasional extraneous remarks, such as "Now let's see," that were excluded from the analysis.

ANALYSIS OF PROBLEM SOLVING UNITS

One of the most intriguing factors was the incredible richness of the process. In instance after instance, the actor appeared to base a large number of decisions regarding interpretation and performance on a mere few words of the script. For example, at one point the character said, "Thanks. Er- thanks." From these few words, the participant:

1. Inferred Austin's mental state, "his mind is preoccupied" (protocol statement # 3).
2. Used the information in a backward chaining fashion to reinterpret a previous line and infer Austin's emotional state at that time (protocol statement # 5).
3. Used the character's stammering as a "clue to the rhythm of his speech" (protocol statement # 30).
4. Extended the previous to include Austin's walk and movement, "I don't think he's fluid in his movements" (protocol statement # 32).
5. Looked for other incidents of Austin's stammering and when he noticed the absence of stammering in one section (protocol statement # 36), used that

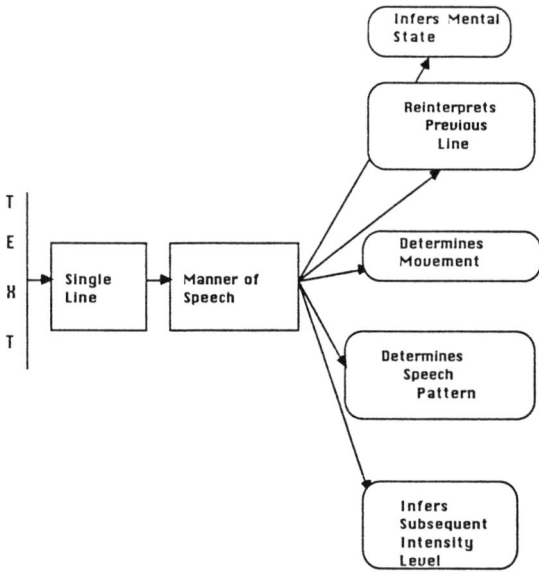

FIG. 6.1. Number of interpretations derived from a single line of text. *Note.* From "An Example of Role Preparation by a Professional Actor: A Think-Aloud Protocol," by H. Noice and T. Noice, 1994, *Discourse Processes, 18*, p. 351. Copyright © 1994 by Ablex Publishing Corporation. Reprinted with permission.

information to infer a change in the intensity level. This information is represented graphically in Fig. 6.1.

All PSUs were broken down into input and output. The former concerned what aspects of the text were attended to; the latter concerned what the participant learned by attending to them. The input was further broken down into content or form and the output into internal characteristics or performance characteristics. The following definitions should make this clear.

Content (C) Versus Form (F)

The rater determined whether the participant attended primarily to the content of the script (e.g., "Obviously by this time we see that Austin is hiding something. He's got some kind of hidden agenda going on," protocol statement # 22), or primarily to the form of the script, (e.g., "There are a lot of monosyllabic words in here, suggesting a very pointed emotional forceful delivery," protocol statement # 37).

When attending to form, the participant appeared to derive character information from the following linguistic components and devices:

1. The existence of plosives, fricatives, and monosyllabic words.
2. Onomatopoeia ("Nice sound, the s-sound, the snake sound," protocol statement # 47).
3. Tempo ("There is speed here, the rhythm has increased its tempo, it's more of an allegro," protocol statement # 40).
4. Punctuation ("The punctuation gives us a clue here. We never get an exclamation point. We never get capitalization," protocol statement # 43).
5. Structure of lines ("His longer line starting with, 'it's rotten to be this way,' is very important because we've got so many clauses in there," protocol statement # 72).

In some cases, the participant attended to both form and content (e.g., "The longer line has a clue in it about what this scene is about, and what this guy's trying to do. Because it is longer, there must be something important in it," problem statements # 18–19). In this instance, the participant was clearly attending to the content (what this scene is about) but at the same time was attending to the form (length).

Specification of Content or Form

Here the rater indicated exactly what part of the input was being attended to. That is, if content, was it a specific line, an entire section, a manner-of-speaking, the progression of a scene, or the stage directions? If form, was the participant attending to punctuation, linguistic cues, rhythm, or length of lines or sections?

Output: Internal Characteristics (IC) Versus Performance Characteristics (PC)

Here the rater determined what the participant derived from the input. Did the participant determine the internal state of the character, (i.e., the thoughts he was thinking or the emotions he was feeling). If so, the utterance was labeled IC. On the other hand, if the participant determined the external aspects of the character, (i.e., how and where the participant would move, or speak, or manipulate the dynamics of the scene by being louder or softer, slower or faster, etc., then the utterance would be labeled PC).

Specification of Internal Characteristics or Performance Characteristics

Here the participant indicated the specifics of what he had learned. If the utterance was categorized as applying to an internal characteristic, what specifically was determined? Was it the character's motivation, intention, or degree of intensity? To be counted as a motivation, the utterance had to concern *why* the character thought or acted as he did (e.g., "Something about her smile, the way she smiles at him, sets him off-guard," protocol statement # 14). To be listed as an intention, the utterance had to concern the plan of the character (e.g., "I can see him trying to *divert* the conversation," protocol statement # 23). To be listed as degree of intensity, the utterance had to concern the relative emotionality of the character's mental or emotional state (e.g., "He asked her abruptly, 'Are you going to marry Storey?' It's another emotional charge there," protocol statement # 68).

If an utterance was characterized as applying to performance characteristics, did it concern the quality or type of movement (Q/T-Mo), the quality or type of speech (Q/T-Sp), or the dynamics of the scene (Dyn)? To be listed as Q/T-Mo, the participant had to describe physical movement (e.g., "I can see him standing back up when he says, 'He hadn't,'" protocol statement # 11). To be listed as Q/T-Sp, the participant had to describe the character's speech pattern (e. g., "By the same, [he] has his nonfluid speech," protocol statement # 33). To be listed as Dyn, the participant had to have described the ebb and flow of the section. For example, "That and the movement of this one seems to start out slowly and peak in the middle of 'see me' and then come back down by the time we get to 'thank you'" (protocol statement # 24).

Some units pertained to both internal and external characteristics. For example: "Whereas on, 'I do,' I think he's probably had to turn away from her on that line," (protocol statement # 88). The participant's use of the word *had* indicated that he believed the character felt *impelled* to turn away. Therefore this utterance looks at both internal characteristics (motivation) and external characteristics (movement). Of course, the participant did not analyze every speech along all these dimensions. Therefore, the rater scored certain categories as *Not Specified* (NS).

Table 6.2 shows the interrelationships of the various problem-solving units that have been characterized along these dimensions. As can be seen, in the majority of the units T. D. attended solely to the content or meaning of the script (49 instances). Furthermore, when he attended to content, he extracted mainly internal characteristics. However, when he attended to content and form simultaneously, he derived twice as many performance characteristics as internal characteristics. When he attended solely to form, more often than not he discussed the nature of the form rather than its application. For example, in protocol statement # 47 he said:

> Again there are some wonderful onomatopoeic things in that last speech after bitterly. "She probably did. It must have taken a long time because when you came, Storey hadn't even begun to dress." Nice sound: the s sound, the snake sound is an onomatopoeic, a wonderful device there.

Although many more PSUs dealt solely with content than solely with form (48 vs. 6), generally speaking, the units that dealt with form were quite

TABLE 6.2

Total Number of PSUs as a Function of Aspect of Text Attended to (Input) and Derived Characteristics (Output)

		Type of Character Analysis			
Input		Output			
Aspects of Text Attended to	Frequency	Internal Charact.	Performance Charact.	Internal & Performance Charact.	N/S
Content	49	36	4	6	3
Form	6	0	1	1	4
Content & form	10	3	6	1	0
Total	65	39	11	8	7

Note. N/S = Not Specified; Charact. = Characteristics. From "An Example of Role Preparation by a Professional Actor: A Think-Aloud Protocol," by H. Noice and T. Noice, 1994, *Discourse Processes, 18,* p. 354. Copyright © 1994 by Ablex Publishing Corporation. Reprinted with permission.

TABLE 6.3

Correspondence Between Input and Output

	Internal Characteristics				Performance Characteristics				
	MOT	INT	ES	DOI	Q/S	Q/M	DYN	N/S	TTL
Content									
Specific line	6	6	2	2	1	4		3	24
Manner of speaking	1		1	1	3	1			7
Progression				1			1	1	3
Stage direction	2	1		1		1			5
Form									
Linguistic cues				1	2			2	5
Rhythm						2	2		4
Length		1						3	4
Punctuation		2			1		1		4
Total	11	22	8	8	9	9	5	11	83

Note. MOT=motivation; INT=intention; ES=emotional state; DOI=degree of intensity; Q/S=quality of speech; Q/M=quality of movement; DYN=dynamics; N/S=not specified; TTL=total. From "An Example of Role Preparation by a Professional Actor: A Think-Aloud Protocol," by H. Noice and T. Noice, 1994, *Discourse Processes, 18*, p. 355. Copyright © 1994 by Ablex Publishing Corporation. Reprinted with permission.

detailed, focusing on very specific aspects of the text (such as the use of onomatopoeia in statement # 47.)

RESULTS OF INQUIRY

To shed light on the nature of the participant's mental processes during the course of problem solving, the next analysis compared the specific aspects of the text he attended to (the input) and the information he derived from them (the output). These data are shown in Table 6.3. It should be noted that, in some cases, in order to determine a single characteristic, the participant attended to two aspects of the text in the same problem-solving unit (e. g., a specific line and a section of text). In other cases, the participant determined both internal and performance characteristics by attending to only one aspect of the text. For this reason, the total number of entries differs from the total number of PSUs.

As can be seen, the greatest number of PSUs were devoted to identifying the assigned character's internal characteristics (49 as opposed to 23 for performance characteristics). Among the three internal characteristics (intention, motivation, degree of intensity), the participant derived the intention twice as often as the next highest internal characteristic, motivation. This pattern of results is indicative of plan recognition behavior and is consistent with our earlier results that an actor teases out the underlying meaning of a text by determining the assigned character's plan.

Under performance characteristics, the participant attended to quality or type of speech and quality or type of movement equally often (9 entries each) and less often to the ebb and flow of the scene in terms of volume or pace (dynamics). There were a total of 11 entries called, "not specified," meaning the information the participant gave was not explicit enough to characterize further. Quite a few times, the participant simply said a particular line or section was important. Because he did not say what was important about it, it was listed as not specified.

Overall, the participant derived much more information from content than from form (66 entries as opposed to 17). Moreover, as might be expected, when looking at content, he primarily derived internal characteristics, and when looking at form he derived primarily performance characteristics.

PROTOCOL DIVISION VERSUS SCRIPT DIVISION

The participant divided the script into six subsections he referred to as "beats." It is important to note that the term "beat" refers to the participant's division of the playscript itself and bears no relation to the experimenters' division of the participant's verbal protocol. The participant made his reasons for these divisions explicit in only a few cases, when he generated organizing statements such as, "That's where the emotion seems to change" (protocol statement # 2). However, this approach of subdividing a script is widely used by actors and has frequently been described by acting theorists (e.g., Glenn, 1977; Grote, 1985; Hagen, 1991; Kirk & Bellas, 1985). By comparing the organizing statements in T. D.'s protocol (Appendix B) with the scene he was analyzing (Appendix A), it is possible to calculate the number of idea units in each beat. The largest beat contained 9 idea units and the smallest 4 with an average of 6.83.

Table 6.4 compares the correspondence between the number of idea units per beat and the number of PSUs T. D. generated. As can be seen, there was no correspondence between size of a beat in terms of the number of idea units in the character's speeches in the original script and the number of PSUs reported in the protocol. Furthermore, the participant appeared to use different analytical approaches in different beats. In Beat 2, he derived much of the information about the interpretation of his own speeches from the speeches of the other character in the scene. That is, the participant analyzed his own lines as responses to what the other character said or did. Most of the time, he attended to the content

TABLE 6.4

Actor's Organization of the Script Into Beats and the Number of PSUs Generated per Beat

Beats	Number of PSUs	Number of Corresponding Idea Units in Original Script
Beat 1	6	6
Beat 2	17	4
Beat 3	8	9
Beat 4	13	7
Beat 5	13	9
Beat 6	8	6
Total	65	41

Note. From "An Example of Role Preparation by a Professional Actor: A Think-Aloud Protocol," by H. Noice and T. Noice, 1994, Discourse Processes, 18, p. 356. Copyright © 1994 by Ablex Publishing Corporation. Reprinted with permission.

of the lines and used that information to infer motivations, intentions, or the emotional life of the character.

In Beat 3, instead of attending mainly to individual lines, he looked at the beat as a whole. When he did look at specific lines, they were those spoken by his assigned character. In addition to analyzing the content, he extracted a great deal of information from linguistic elements or punctuation. Furthermore, he used the input to derive both internal and performance characteristics. A comparison of the specific problems solved in Beat 2 and Beat 3 is shown in Fig. 6.2.

What was most striking is that totally different problem-solving approaches were used for the two beats. This might possibly be explained by the fact that many playwriting theorists and teachers consider it advisable for playwrights to devote certain sections of text primarily to revealing character and other sections to advancing the plot (e.g., Smiley, 1971). As an analysis of the original script revealed, the lines designated by the participant as Beat 2 deal primarily with character (examining the reasons for Austin's feelings of unease), whereas Beat 3 deals with plot (revealing the discovery of a scarf belonging to Austin's girlfriend in another man's apartment). It is therefore not surprising that the participant regarded that section of the script as containing two separate beats, one concerning character and the other concerning plot, and that he derived more information from the former than the latter. (For a complete discussion of this type of script segmentation as revealed by empirical investigation, see chap. 9.)

A Think-Aloud Protocol

Beat 2

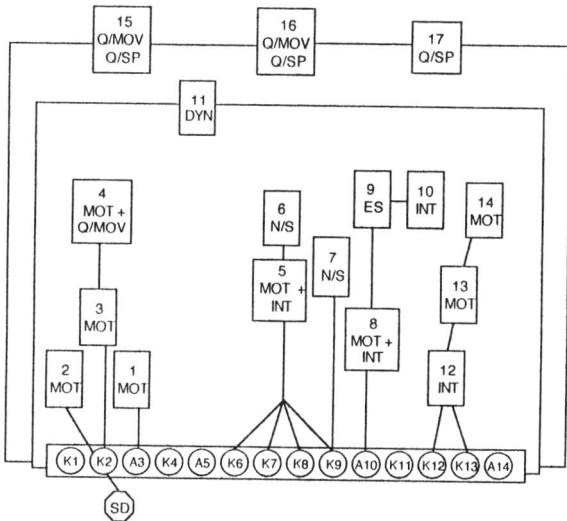

Beat 3

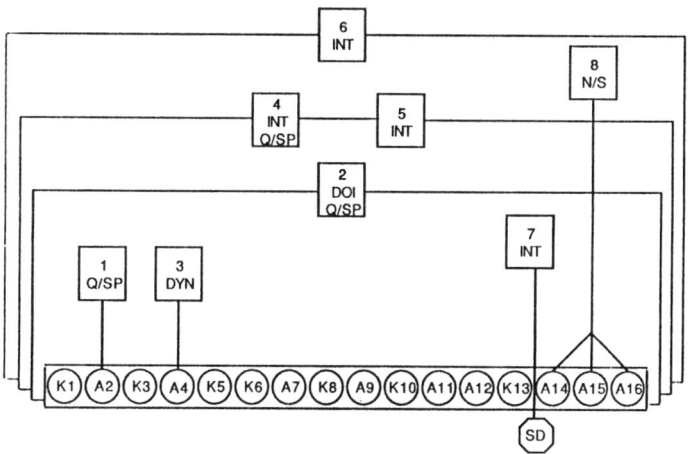

FIG. 6.2. Comparison of subject's problem solving strategies in Beats 2 and 3. *Note.* The small circles denote all idea units of Kendall (K) and Austin (A) in Beats 2 and 3. The information in the boxes gives the order of the protocol statements as well as its output. DOI = Degree of intensity; DYN = Dynamics; ES = Emotional state; INT = Intention; MOT = Motivation; Q/MOV = Quality of movement; Q/SP = Quality of speech; SD = Stage direction; N/S = Not specified. From "An Example of Role Preparation by a Professional Actor: A Think-Aloud Protocol," by H. Noice and T. Noice, 1994, *Discourse Processes, 18,* p. 357. Copyright © 1994 by Ablex Publishing Corporation. Reprinted with permission.

RELIABILITY OF CODING

The classification scheme was devised by both authors. An independent rater was then trained by the first author using actual examples. Agreement in classification was: for content 98.33%; for specification of content 98.33%; for form 100%; for specification of form 94.12%; for internal characteristics 93.88%; for specification of internal characteristics 93.88%; for performance characteristics 82.61%; and for specification of performance characteristics 86.96%. Any disagreements were resolved by the second author.

ACTOR'S METACOGNITION

Although our main interest was in the analysis of the PSUs, the actor's own description of his metacognition shed additional light on the process. The whole issue of the value of elaboration for memory is nicely rendered in protocol statements # 73 and # 74 where he says, "We need to differentiate between each clause in some way so that they aren't the same and have the same content. Because you can't memorize them with all the same content; otherwise it's just rote learning" (protocol statement # 73); and "the more context you have, the faster you memorize it, and the more natural it comes out" (protocol statement # 74). In protocol statement # 81, he says, "And that's something I will remember immediately. There is no problem to memorize [it] because it has such an emotional content to it."

T. D. lucidly summarized his preparation process in his closing comments starting with protocol statement # 92 that included such comments as, "The more clues, cues, memory cues I can provide myself ... the easier it is to learn, the more natural it will seem." The actor specifically credited his isolation of the various mental, emotional, and physical cues as a prelude to memorizing the material.

DISCUSSION

This study provides a detailed picture of the mental processes of one particular actor during the early stages of role preparation. The retrospective protocols described in chapter 2, while presenting an excellent overview, averaged only 25 elaborations each. The participant in the present study, using a think-aloud procedure, generated almost 100 elaborations that not only corroborated but extended the results of our original protocols.

Once again, the majority of elaborations were concerned with determining the character's plan-fulfilling actions and attributes. However, analysis of this think-aloud protocol showed not only the existence of these elaborations but the process by which they were derived. In addition to the underlying meaning, T. D. attended to a multitude of other cues to determine various internal and external aspects of the character, focusing on linguistic information, punctuation, manner-of-speaking, parenthetical material, and structure.

Before performing this in-depth analysis, the participant appeared to isolate the section, or "beat," he was going to work on. Within each beat, the actor did not appear to go through a mental checklist but simply derived whatever information the material itself seemed to offer. That is, the actor did not appear to have a number of slots that he sought to instantiate sequentially, but rather he derived his elaborations from the nature of the input. In some beats, he focused predominantly on the meaning of specific lines or sections. In other beats, he attended predominantly to parenthetical comments, punctuation, linguistic information, or the rhythm of the text. At no time did the participant proceed in exactly the same manner as the time before, indicating an absence of a predetermined, mechanically implemented strategy. It is, of course, possible that he had a specific metastrategy for selecting from a repertoire of potential strategies, but no indication of this was found. Rather, the participant appeared to respond to the input, using whatever strategy seemed appropriate at the moment. Also, he not only worked forward but often engaged in backtracking, using the interpretation of a new line to reinterpret a previous one.

Within each beat the participant's analysis appeared to be a two-stage process. The actor first dug out the information from various aspects of the text; then he used that information to infer the nature of the character he was to portray and the specific performance attributes by which he would communicate those qualities to an audience.

When inferring the intentions and motivations of the characters, the participant often appeared to ask "why" questions of the script. "Why" questions have been shown to facilitate both comprehension and retention (e.g., Pressley, McDaniel, Turnure, Wood, & Ahmad, 1987; Pressley, Symons, McDaniel, Snyder, & Turnure, 1988; Stein & Bransford, 1979; Stein, Littlefield, Bransford, & Persampieri, 1984; Woloshyn, Willoughby, Wood, & Pressley, 1990). For example, Pressley et al. (1988) specifically required participants to answer so-called "why" questions following the presentation of a factual statement. This manipulation resulted in increased learning, probably due to the extensive analysis participants had to carry out to answer the question precisely. Apparently, having to state why a particular fact was true forced participants to supply elaborations that reduced arbitrariness between concepts in a sentence, and this type of elaborative interrogation seemed to promote learning.

In examining the role of questioning during comprehension, Trabasso and Magliano (1996) had college students generate think-aloud protocols while they read eight stories, each containing three episodes. In analyzing these protocols, the investigators found three types of utterances: explanations, associations, and predictions. When the participants' comments were in the form of answers to "why" questions, they appeared to function as *explanations*; when the utterances were answers to "what, how, where, when, and who" questions, they seemed to function as *associations*; and when they were answers to causal consequence questions, they seemed to function as *predictions*. By far the greatest number of inferences were categorized as explanations. Even though only 13% of the sentences in the original stories contained references to goals, the most frequent type of explanation was goal-based, providing support for the notion that goal assignment is an indispensable aspect of the comprehension of narratives. Summing up the results from this and other pertinent research (e.g., Chi et al., 1989; Graesser, Singer, & Trabasso, 1994; Trabasso, van den Broek, & Suh, 1989), Trabasso and Magliano (1996) concluded that, "The predominance of explanation-based inferences in thinking aloud is consistent with other behavioral evidence" (p. 283).

T. D.'s think-aloud protocol provides still another instance in which the emphasis is strongly on explaining the actions of the characters. Our participant's manner of questioning appears to be akin to the concept of self-explanations as advanced by Chi and VanLehn (1991). In their view, "Self-explanations are generated in the context of learning something new, whereas elaborations generally refer to the use of existing knowledge to embed or embellish a piece of information in a larger context so that it is more memorable" (pp. 71-72). Chi et al. (1989) showed that the use of self-explanation is one characteristic that distinguishes students who are good problem solvers from those who are not. Similarly, the study described in chapter 3 (Noice, 1991) showed that professional actors seek far more explanations of the character's actions than novices do when studying the same text.

This think-aloud protocol also revealed that the participant paid great attention to lines spoken by the other character in the scene, focusing on how truthful the other character's statements were and how they affected his own plans. This attention to intersecting plans and belief systems has been identified as one of the components underlying comprehension (Bruce, 1975; Bruce & Newman, 1978; Miller, 1973). The participant's attention to the other character's lines may also be explained by the fact that a playscript is a representation of spoken discourse and differs from written discourse in several important ways. It has been shown that human conversation operates within a framework of tacit knowledge of various rules, regulations, and conventions of spoken discourse, with participants exchanging information by a nod of the head, smiles, or the averting of one's eyes. Other signals are interrupting, trailing off in midsentence, and making leading statements (Grice, 1975; Searle, 1976). The protocol shows that the participant was acutely aware of all of these pragmatic aspects of communication. Throughout, it was obvious that the participant examined the written text for the purpose of turning it into living conversation.

This protocol also revealed the redundancy in the participant's preparation of a role. In addition to attending to the literal words, he speculated on the deep meaning, the emotional tone, and the tempo for the scene. He also visualized the setting, placing the actors in different positions on stage, charting their movements and, more importantly, advancing explanations for those movements. These procedures appeared to result in a number of codes in various modalities. This redundancy in the mental representation of information has been shown to make memory more enduring (e.g., Anderson & Reder, 1979; Paivio, 1971).

No claim is made that all actors presented with the same script would be equally competent in terms of metacognition or would proceed in an identical fashion. Indeed, this participant was selected because he appeared to be highly articulate. Therefore, this protocol is probably more explicit than one that might be derived from an actor who was less expert at putting his thoughts into words. However, because our previous research indicated that this overall type of analysis is in general use among professional actors, the purpose of this protocol analysis was to examine in detail how one particular actor formed a mental representation of a text. The view that emerged provides a concrete example of a learning strategy that may enhance comprehension and retention across a number of content areas. This is in line with research that views understanding as requiring "different kinds of knowledge *not* explicitly referred to in the text or problem solution, as well as strategies for governing how this implicit knowledge should be used in synthesizing a structural model of the meaning of the text or problem solution" (Brown et al., 1978, p. 108). The depth of understanding revealed by this protocol appears to be one of the factors behind the ability of actors to remember hundreds of lines of complex material in real time, verbatim, and with relative ease.

So far, the studies in this series indicate that actors acquire a verbatim representation of the text by employing a strategy that primarily results in gist recall. While we have speculated on various factors that might be involved in this phenomenon, no single definitive explanation has emerged. However, the interviews, the retrospective protocols, and the one online protocol all seem to point to the conclusion that the actor's process requires such close attention to the exact wording of the script (for the purpose of gaining clues to interpretation), that none of the words seem arbitrary. That is, an actor's elaborations concern not just the ideas in question but the reasons for expressing those ideas by using those particular words.

As an anecdotal example, in the play, *The Front Page* (Hecht & McArthur, 1949) the mayor says to a reporter: "Don't pester me now, please." The actor inferred from the use of the word *pester* that the mayor thought of the reporter as a bothersome child since the term is frequently used with children. We conjecture that this elaboration would necessarily make the term *pester* memorable. That is, an actor would not inadvertently substitute annoy or bother or any other synonym because he had specifically attended to the exact word *pester* and had come up with a reason why that character would use that word and not some other. Furthermore, the mayor, not wanting to alienate a reporter, softens the statement by adding, "please." In addition, the egotistical mayor might be proud of his use of alliteration, further ensuring recall of the line, "Don't pester me now, please."

CONCLUSION

This think-aloud protocol revealed that this actors' approach to script analysis brings together in a concentrated and specific manner a number of factors that have been shown to influence comprehension and learning. Furthermore, a comparison of this participant's metastatements with his problem-solving statements demonstrates a close correspondence between the participant's description of his procedure and his actual working methods. We feel that it is this type of microscopic examination of the exact wording that produces verbatim results with a learning strategy that normally only produces recall of the gist.

However, the retrospective protocols of the early experiments were not detailed enough to confirm this, and this one in-depth, think-aloud protocol might have been atypical. Therefore, additional think-aloud protocols were needed to confirm whether this minute attention to the exact wording of the text is a defining feature of many actors' memory process. These protocols were collected, and the analysis of them is reported in chapter 7.

7

More Think-Aloud Protocols

New protocols were collected from six additional male actors with at least 10 years of professional experience, none of whom had ever performed the play *The Second Man* (Behrman, 1952) from which our test scene was taken (Noice & Noice, 1996a). The actors were instructed to read the scene over once to see what it was about, then to go back to the beginning and start studying as if they were preparing for a performance. They were specifically instructed to use whatever procedures they normally would if this were their first session with a script that they would eventually perform from memory. Participants were asked not to censor anything, but to verbalize their thoughts as they proceeded line by line through the script. All of the tapes were then transcribed for analysis.

CODING

With the original retrospective protocols, we had used a fairly wide categorization scheme in order to gain an overall picture of actors' mental processes. At this point, we wished to get a much more detailed picture without repeating the exhaustive analysis characteristic of our single-actor study. An examination of the new protocols revealed that all utterances consisted of either exploring the content of the playscript or explaining the participants' methods of approaching the learning of it. In either case, each utterance was in the nature of an explanation and therefore we used, as a unit of analysis, what we termed an explanatory unit (EU). These EUs ranged from a single sentence to a full page, but regardless of length, they were devoted to a single aspect of analysis. Furthermore, we sorted these units into 12 categories.

1. *Background.* Statements speculating on or investigating such factors as location, time of day, occupations of the characters, etc.
2. *Interactions.* Statements concerning mental or emotional interactions between characters in which one character affects, tries to affect or is affected by another character. Also categorized in this manner are state-

ments regarding interactions between the character and characters not present in the scene but talked about.

3. *Traits*. Statements regarding enduring character traits, such as shyness or sophistication.

4. *Importance*. Statements regarding the relative importance of particular lines because they summed up a situation or revealed the specific nature of an interaction.

5. *Memorization*. Statements regarding the relative ease or difficulty of learning certain lines and/or the reasons why particular lines would be memorable. This category contained five subcategories: references to events that had actually occurred previously onstage; exchanges in which the cue line would usually trigger the response (e. g., *Cue*: "Now you're angry." Response: "Of course I'm angry."); visualization of events that did not occur onstage but were referred to in the dialogue; extraction of underlying meaning before memorization; and lines being prompted by movements such as saying "Hello" after shaking hands.

6. *Response/Initiative*. Statements noting whether a particular line or section was a response to the other character's preceding line or the introduction of new subject matter.

7. *Linguistic Information*. Statements that focused on such elements as length or sound of words or speeches.

8. *Performance Aspects*. Statements regarding how the subject would use the information in the script to enhance performance.

9. *Style*. Statements focusing on or speculating on the style of language, the era of the play, the genre of the play, the playwright's other works, etc.

10. *Directorial Input*. Statements regarding interpretation of lines or sections that might change based on the director's eventual choice.

11. *Metastatements*. Statements regarding a subject's process of learning a script in general without reference to this particular scene.

12. *Editorial/Extraneous*. Statements that do not refer to the script at all but are simply peripheral comments.

Table 7.1 presents examples of participants' protocol statements that would fit into each of these 12 categories. The two authors analyzed all of the protocols independently and their agreement was 89%. Then, as a check of reliability, a randomly selected subset of 50% was scored by an independent rater. The mean percentage of agreement between the independent judge and the authors was 87.11%. All differences were resolved through discussion.

A total of 462 explanatory units was generated. The shortest protocol contained 31 and the longest 98 ($M = 77$). The classification of these units into the 12 categories listed is shown in Table 7.2. As Table 7.2 shows, all actors attended primarily to mental and emotional interactions with other

TABLE 7.1

Example of Each Category Type in Actors' Think-Aloud Protocols

Classification	Examples
Background	One wants to be very aware of the world at the time, at the events of the play, of the relationships, of what's already been established.
Interactions	"There's something funny about most things." That leads me to a feeling that, well, why don't I seek help from this woman. Why don't I trust her with my feeling.
Traits	I think that's what shows me what he is; the scientist in him, and even with somewhat of a sense of humor.
Importance	Now she gives me information,,"I was here promptly at eleven. Storey hadn't even begun to dress." And I say, "He hadn't!" with an exclamation point. That exclamation point tells me that this is something very important.
Memorization	She asks me, "Do you know what time it is?" I look at the watch, "Ten minutes past eleven." That's certainly going to be easy to remember. She just tells me what my line is by asking me what time it is.
Responsive/initiative	Next line is again tentative. I repeat myself. "I'm glad I found you." Again it's response.
Linguistic information	I noticed the words are longer. We have polysyllabic words. They tend to have a more singing quality to them
Performance aspects	"Cigarette, thanks." Perhaps she offers him one and the second thanks is actually on getting it. So, there seems to be a possibility for some sort of physical contact or at least both people touching the same cigarette.
Style	You know to me, it's very important how things fit into context. Indeed, that sort of mysterious word "style," you know, what kind of a world are we in? Is this a comedy, is this a mystery, is this a soap opera, what is the world?
Directorial input	Kendall offers me a cigarette. I wonder if the director will change that. If he's updating it...an awful lot of them have given up smoking.
Metastatements	You know, finding out the essential differences in a genre piece or a style piece is to me very important when one is beginning the work.
Editorial/extraneous	Ah, the connections aren't real clear as I read through this.

characters. In these statements, actors constantly appeared to be probing what was said in order to determine what the character really meant. That is, the protocol statements concerned such speculations as the character possibly using the words as a smoke screen to conceal his real feelings, or laying his cards on the table, or trying to make up his mind. A typical statement categorized as an interaction was:

And she says, "Well then— ?" Now she's asking me to explore the issue further by saying, "Well then—?" And now I might as well tell her what's bothering me, "She wore it when I left with her." Well, if she wore it when I left with her and it's here now and she's not here yet, then obviously she came back to see him. Or she came back for some reason and if I'm insecure about my fiancee's love, well, I could easily think that she came back to see Storey. (Noice & Noice, 1996, p. 7)

Over 40% of EUs (in all 12 categories combined) concerned this one category: mental or emotional interactions. This compares to 8.87% for metastatements, the next highest category. This finding is obviously very much in keeping with our previous findings. However, while these actors' statements regarding script learning revealed many areas of commonality, they also revealed many areas of difference. That is, although the primary area of emphasis for all actors was on mental or emotional interactions, the secondary areas of emphasis varied greatly. For example, overall, only 3.9% of the statements concerned enduring character traits, 7.14% concerned the relationship between the script and the actors' eventual performance, and less than 0.5% discussed linguistic aspects of the text or the probable input of the director. It is particularly interesting that, since the experimental instructions specifically asked the actors to study the script as if it were

TABLE 7.2

Classification of Actors' Explanatory Units (in Percentages)

	Actors						
	A. A.	T. D.	B. G.	A. N.	P. T.	S. W.	MEAN
Background	6.25		3.57	2.04	12.37	12.05	6.06
Interactions	40.63	40.63	35.71	59.18	43.30	27.71	42.21
Traits	6.25		5.36		10.31	3.61	3.90
Importance	12.5	16.67	10.71	2.04		2.41	6.49
Memorization	32.25	2.08		23.47		6.02	8.66
Response/initiative	3.13			1.02	21.65		4.98
Linguistic information		2.08					.43
Performance		13.54	12.5	3.06	2.06	9.64	7.14
Style			12.5	3.09		12.05	4.33
Directorial input				2.04			.43
Metastatements		17.71	1.79	5.10	1.03	20.48	8.87
Editorial comments		7.29	17.86	2.04	6.19	6.02	6.49
Total number of EUs:	32	96	56	98	97	83	462

Note. From "Two Approaches to Learning a Theatrical Script," by H. Noice and T. Noice, 1996, Memory, 4, p. 7. Copyright © 1996 by Erlbaum (UK) Taylor and Francis. Reprinted with permission.

their first study session with a text that they would have to perform from memory, only 8.66% of the explanatory units concerned memorization of the script. (However an additional 8.87% of the utterances were metastatements, often concerning the participants' general processes of memorization without reference to the particular scene being studied.)

We were particularly interested in determining whether all actors probed the script at a microlevel to extract performance information from the dialogue, punctuation, etc. If evidence were found for this, it would support our hypothesis that actors' fine-grained analysis of the script is responsible for their obtaining word-for-word recall with a strategy that usually delivers only recall of the gist. Evidence was found that every actor repeatedly used this sort of analysis. The following list gives but one example from each actor's protocol:

- S. W., referring to the line, "Ten minutes past eleven," said, "it's sort of interesting the relative accuracy of that in a predigital world.... He doesn't say it's just past eleven or a little after eleven. He's pretty exact about it."
- About the line, "Yes, I did," P. T. said, "I don't say anything more than I need to say. Short answers."
- B. G. noted, "In the way the characters behave and act toward one another, it's, it's very much—it strikes me 1930s, 1940s. There's a grandness to the language."
- P. T. referring to the line, "He hadn't!" said, "with an exclamation mark—explanation point, one of surprise."
- A. N., referring to the line, "Er ... thanks. Thanks," said, "trying to be cool and man-of-the worldish, but I stutter a little."
- A. A. referring to the line, "Why should I care if Monica came back here or not? And yet ... I do," said, "this line is essentially all of Austin's internal monologue and it finally becomes, rather than the subtext, it becomes the actual text."

Every actor's protocol contained numerous examples of this textual examination at the word and phrase level, in order to make more global judgments about character and situation.

CONCLUSION

Virtually all of the actors' utterances were explanation-based, regardless of the categories into which they fitted. For example, the statement, "That leads me to a feeling that, well, why don't I seek help from this woman," and the statement, "Is this a comedy, is this a mystery, is this a soap opera, what is the world?" are both explanations. However, the former is in the nature of an *interaction* whereas the latter concerns the play's *style*. It has frequently been suggested (e.g., Graesser et al., 1994) that generating explanatory elaborations is an essential component of the comprehension process. However, the elaborations generated in this study indicated that the actors went further than just comprehending the text; they used their explanations to infer unstated ideas that, although not necessary for literal understanding, were important for creating a well-rounded character who would choose those words to gain his or her ends.

Although this study clearly revealed commonalities between various actors' script-learning processes, some individual differences stood out. These differences suggest a number of additional research questions. One such question concerns the comparative speed or durability of learning by different actors based on their tendency to generate particular types of elaborations. Because we have repeatedly found that actors tend to think primarily about interactions with other characters, might their secondary and tertiary areas of emphasis (which vary greatly) differentially affect their role acquisition? Another question concerns the generalizability of these results to other areas of performance expertise, such as piano playing and figure skating, that do not use language but involve extensive physical practice.

We have already obtained preliminary evidence that there is a connection between actors' verbal and motoric representations of a role (Noice, 1992), and some new research into this area is discussed in chapter 12. For the time being, we would like to point out that these protocols provide converging evidence that actors' script-learning procedures are markedly different from those usually employed for intentional memorization. These differences are further explored in the next chapter by comparing these six actors' learning processes with those of a professional mnemonist.

8

A Mnemonist's Approach to Script Learning

Spectators are amazed when a professional mnemonist, such as Harry Lorayne, correctly identifies every person in an audience of hundreds after having heard their names only once shortly before the performance. Furthermore, audience members verify that the information they supply to the mnemonist (names, social security numbers, telephone numbers, etc.) is precisely remembered (e .g., Wilding & Valentine, 1985, 1994). The research described in previous chapters has shown that actors' recall is also quite accurate. However, even though mnemonists and actors recall to-be-remembered material verbatim, the material itself is very different. The actor recalls lengthy connected discourse; the mnemonist recalls large numbers of individual items.

At first glance, it would appear that there is little in common between actors' strategies as we uncovered them in our research and mnemonists' strategies as described in books such as *Super Memory—Super Student* (Lorayne, 1990) and *The Memory Book* (Lorayne & Lucas, 1974). However, this could not be said with certainty because the methods a mnemonist might use to learn a theatrical script word-for-word have never been described in detail. Therefore, a study was performed to determine if there are any areas of commonalities between actors' strategies and those a professional mnemonist might use when learning the same theatrical scene verbatim.

It is obvious that the analytical approach of actors differs radically from the imagery/association methods employed during mnemonic demonstrations and described in self-help books on memory improvement. This is not to say that actors never use imagery. Indeed, they frequently visualize entire scenes not in the script in order to flesh out their understanding of the characters or situation, but this is far removed from the application of a mnemonic device such as to buy milk and tomatoes by visualizing milk being poured out of a tomato. However, at least one well known actress, Anne Bancroft, has been quoted as saying that during script learning she does use the mnemonic methods taught by Lorayne (1985), "My most recent play would not have opened had not your systems made it possible for me to memorize an almost impossible-to-memorize script" (Lorayne, 1985, p. 63). Therefore, the Lorayne method must be capable of handling complex discourse as well as discrete items. To examine how this approach might differ from the one favored by our actors, we asked Lorayne to also generate a think-aloud protocol using the same script.

It should be emphasized that theatrical scripts are almost always committed to memory over an entire rehearsal period that runs at least 2 weeks and often 4 or more, and that even Lorayne, whose demonstrations routinely consist of recalling material after only a single exposure, advises those who need to learn scripts that, in addition to his visualize-and-link approach, they should go over the material many, many times (Lorayne, 1957, 1985). Therefore (as with the six actors described in the last chapter), Lorayne was not asked to memorize the script, but rather to go through a single pass of the five pages trying to simultaneously verbalize all his thoughts. What was important to us was not how much he, or the actors, retained from one detailed read-through (because they always do repeated read-throughs), but what the process was during learning.

The methodology of mnemonists has been extensively reviewed in the psychological literature (e.g., Bellezza, 1981; Bower, 1970; Higbee, 1988; see also Herrmann, 1991). One of the most frequently used approaches is to form images for the to-be-remembered facts and link them together so as to form a single combined image. For example, to remember church and vacuum cleaners, one might visualize the interior of a church with the pews filled with vacuum cleaners rather than parishioners. For each additional to-be-remembered item, a new picture is formed linking the new item to the last remembered item.

Another approach consists of prememorizing a list of "peg" words to which material is linked. One well known example is "one is a bun, two is a shoe, three is a tree," and so forth. If the first to-be-remembered item is a pen, the mnemonist might picture a pen instead of a hamburger on a bun. Recalling bun would bring back the image of the pen. A more complex peg-word system has been referred to as analytic substitution (Loisette, 1899; see also Norman, 1976) or the figure alphabet (cf. Gordon, Valentine, & Wilding, 1984). Here each digit is represented by a consonant sound (e.g., $t = 1$, $n = 2$, $m = 3$). Peg words are built from these sounds using whatever additional vowels (or consonants not in the figure alphabet) are necessary to construct visualizable words. Thus, the digit 1 could be represented by tie (or toe, or tea, etc); 2 could be represented by Noah; 3 by Ma; 12 by tin; 13 by team, and so forth. In addition to constructing peg words, mnemonists use this device to remember addresses, dates, telephone numbers, etc.

Mnemonic devices such as these have also been employed to aid retention of speeches and prose paragraphs (e.g., Gruneberg, 1978; Krebs, Snowman, & Smith, 1978; Snowman, Krebs, & Lockhart, 1980). However, in those situations only the main ideas are coded, which later serve as retrieval cues for reconstructing the gist of the speech or passage. Our interest was in how an expert mnemonist would encode complex material that must be retained word-for-word, and how this process would compare to actors' learning strategies.

It was considered essential in this experiment to inform the participants that there would not be a subsequent memory test because, if they were expecting one, they might modify their natural strategies to comply with what they perceived as task demands. This enabled us to compare, on a line by line basis, the mental processes involved during the first pass-through of a theatrical script. The amount and accuracy of recall of the same script was addressed in previous studies (see chaps. 4, 9, and 10).

THE LORAYNE PROTOCOL

In analyzing Lorayne's protocol, it became obvious that it consisted of two sequential parts, describing two totally different strategies. The first part dealt solely with learning the names, appearances, and relationships of the characters described in prose on the first page of the script. The second part of the protocol described how Lorayne would learn the dialogue and connect it with the cue word of each preceding speech.

As with the actors' data, we segmented the protocol into individual units, each devoted to a description of the method Lorayne used to learn a particular amount of material. For the introductory prose portion, he grouped facts together into what he considered logical units (e.g., a person's first and last name; a person's name and his appearance). For the dialogue portion he always associated the line or speech he was to recall with the preceding cue word of the other character. The protocol contained a total of 50 explanatory units, 7 concerning the introductory information and 28 concerning the dialogue portion. In addition, there were 15 statements not concerned with the script itself. Four of these were metastatements about his methods in general and 11 were simply extraneous comments. An example of each type is presented in Table 8.1.

Throughout the protocol, Lorayne appeared to use not only well-known mnemonic techniques (such as visualizing and linking), but an original variation that we call the "miniscenario." In terms of the former, whereas most previous studies of mnemonists' methods have not differentiated between different types of linked images, we wished to take a closer look at the process and found the following forms:

1. *Interactive Image (II)*: Two images, each representing one item, are linked (e.g, an Austin car was wearing a top hat to indicate that the character whose name was Austin was in formal attire).

Table 8.1

Illustrative Examples of Lorayne Protocol

Introductory Portion

Factual information in prose introduction	Then I pictured a large clock being a story high to give me the name of the character that is not even in the scene, Clarke Storey.

Dialogue Portion

Mnemonic device for connecting cue with response	The next line ended with "Ms. Grey." What I thought of was somebody was talking about my grey hair, "What lovely grey hair you have." And I was saying, "Thank you." That's what gave me the "Thank you" line from "Grey."
Metastatement	When I hear the word see, like whenever I'm memorizing a magazine and when anything has to do with see, I visualize binoculars. That's sort of my word for see.
Extraneous comment	See, I thought maybe these things would be interesting for you.

2. *Incorporated Attribute (IA)*: An image is expanded or altered to contain an additional attribute (e.g., to remember the name Clarke Storey, Lorayne visualized a clock, clock=Clarke, that was as tall as a one-story building.)
3. *Action Added (AA)*: A visualizable item is seen performing an action that represents one part of the to-be-remembered information (e. g., the name Kendall Frayne was represented by the image of a candle, candle = Kendall, and by the action of candles raining down, rain=Frayne). All of the mnemonic devices used to code the introductory prose material were of these types.

For the dialogue portion of the script, Lorayne changed strategies. He primarily used a scenario-type device, weaving a ministory out of visualizable transformations. There were two types of these scenarios.

Mini-Scenario (MS1). Here, Lorayne visualized a scene in which the events themselves coded the salient words of the to-be-remembered dialogue. For example, a cue line was, "Well, she probably ran back to tell Storey something," and the character's response was, "She probably did. It must taken a long time because when you came, Storey hadn't even begun to dress." Lorayne transformed the key word in the cue line (Storey) into the image he used whenever the script referred to the character of Clarke Storey, i. e., a clock, one story high. To code the first part of the response ("She [Monica] probably did. It must have taken a long time ... "), Lorayne pictured a harmonica (harmonica = Monica), talking to the clock for a long time, going on and on and on. To code the second part ["because when you (Kendall) came ..."], he saw a candle (candle = Kendall) arriving. To code the remaining part ("Storey hadn't even begun to dress"), Lorayne saw a lot of clothing lying next to the story-high clock.

Mini-Scenario (MS2). Here, Lorayne visualized a scene in which the to-be-remembered dialogue would be a logical response to the coded content of the scene. For example, a cue line was, "and bring Ms. Grey" and the to-be-remembered line was, "Thank you." Lorayne said he imagined that he was having a conversation with someone who said to him, "What lovely gray hair you have." Normally his response would be, "Thank you." So the line about Ms. Grey would effectively cue "Thank you."

These two categories were devised after repeatedly reading the protocol for commonalities. However, Lorayne did not assign these labels; he simply described each mental picture as he generated it. Table 8.2 shows the distribution of these various types of linked images. As can be seen, in coding the prose material that served to introduce the scene, Lorayne relied exclusively on the types of devices frequently employed by mnemonists to learn factual material (Interactive images, Incorporated attributes, Actions added). However, when coding the dialogue, he predominantly used the device we call the miniscenario.

In terms of number of links, although the coding of the prose material invariably involved linking two images, the coding of the dialogue using miniscenarios involved linking from two to five images.

In only one case (when referring to a cigarette) did Lorayne actually visualize the item itself; in all other cases, he employed transformations. In the prose material, 79% of these transformations were phonetic (e.g., candle for Kendall) and the remainder semantic (e.g., binoculars for the word "see"). In the dialogue portion, the pattern was reversed: 27% of the

TABLE 8.2

Distribution of Types of Imagery Used and Number of Items in Each Image or Scenario

Number of items linked	Prose Introduction			Dialogue				
	II	IA	AA	II	IA	AA	MS1	MS2
2	1	2	4	1	1	2		1
3							6	5
4							3	2
5							4	1
Total	1	2	4	1	1	2	13	9

Note. II = Interactive image; IA = Incorporated attribute; AA = Action added; MS1 = Miniscenario 1; MS2 = Miniscenario 2. From "Two Approaches to Learning a Theatrical Script," by H. Noice and T. Noice, 1996a, *Memory, 4*, p. 11. Copyright © 1996 by Erlbaum (UK) Taylor & Francis. Reprinted with permission.

transformations were phonetic and 73% were semantic. (In four instances, Lorayne did not describe the image he generated to code a particular item.)

COMPARISON BETWEEN MNEMONIST AND ACTORS

We compared Lorayne's protocol with those generated by the six actors, as described in chapter 7. Lorayne spoke fluently and rapidly with virtually no pauses; the actors were slightly less fluent, often pausing to formulate their thoughts. In terms of length, Lorayne's protocol ran 22 minutes and the actors' protocols averaged 24 minutes, with Lorayne generating 50 units and the actors generating an average of 77. Another difference was that about one fifth of Lorayne's explanatory units concerned learning the information given in the script prior to the first line of dialogue: the who, what, where, and when. Actors seemed to plunge right into the dialogue, probing the lines for cues to the character's intentions. Thus Lorayne appeared to look at the script from the outside, as information to be remembered; the actors appeared to look at it from the inside, as a life to be lived.

In terms of variety of encoding devices, Lorayne employed the same strategy throughout: visualize and link (sometimes referred to as imagery mediation; Herrmann, 1987). Actors used a wide variety of analytical strategies, and on those rare occasions when they did mention visualization, it was always within the context of the dramatic situation. For example, referring to Austin's line, "She probably did. It must have taken a long time because when you came, Storey hadn't even begun to dress," actor A. A. said, "He's still responding to events that occurred directly with him and Monica. So all of that I would need to visualize completely, and then it's very easy to memorize the lines."

Figure 8.1 shows the emphasis given to the various aspects of script analysis by the six actors and to mnemonic devices by Lorayne. (Because metastatements and extraneous comments did not deal with learning this particular script, they were disregarded in this analysis.) As Fig. 8.1 shows, all actors were primarily concerned with Category 2: mental or emotional interactions between characters. It might be thought that Category 2 was possibly more inclusive than other categories and therefore the high number of comments in that area was due to this inclusiveness, rather than to the nature of actors' role-learning strategies. However, in previous research (Noice, 1991) it was shown that actors generated approximately twice as many elaborations classified as interactions as novices whereas novices, produced approximately twice as many statements classified as extraneous/editorial as actors. Thus, it appears that expertise is more a determinant of the number of statements produced in each category than is the nature of the categories themselves. Moreover, actors had little in common with one another in terms of their secondary area of emphasis. In contrast,

A Mnemonist's Approach to Script Learning

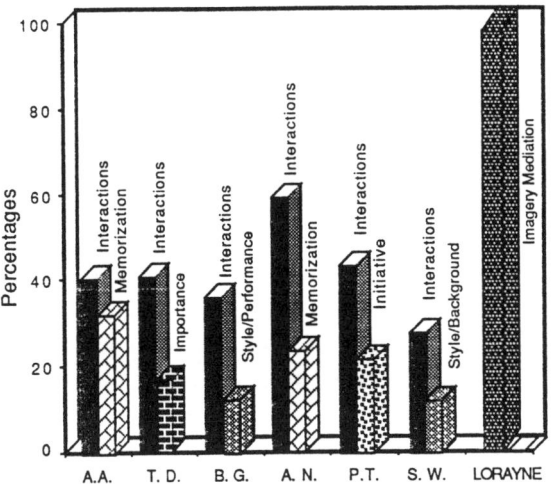

FIG. 8.1. The two most frequently used analytical strategies by six actors (A. A., T. D., B. G., A. N., P. T., and S. W.) and one mnemonist (Lorayne). From "Two Approaches to Learning a Theatrical Script," by H. Noice and T. Noice, 1996a, *Memory, 4*, p. 12. Copyright © 1996 by Erlbaum (UK) Taylor & Francis. Reprinted with permission.

Lorayne had no secondary area of emphasis; all his units concerned imagery mediation.

DISCUSSION

This comparison between actors and a mnemonist produced three main findings.

1. Actors process material at a microlevel in order to derive information essential to role interpretation. Although the actor's strategy is directed toward deriving the deep meaning of the text, the process involves attending to the exact words (e. g., the example in chap. 7 concerning the mayor's use of the word *pester*). This strategy brings into play such psychological factors as effortful processing, elaboration, causality, and plan recognition and appears to explain why actors retain the dialogue verbatim using a meaning-based strategy that normally results only in retention of the gist. The data presented here indicate that, in the course of deriving the meaning of the text, actors devote the same type of minute attention to the individual words that a mnemonist like Lorayne does when he examines them in order to create semantic and phonetic transformations.

2. Lorayne is able to use imagery mediation, a strategy generally thought suitable only for discrete items, to encode the exact wording of text.

3. Comparing Lorayne's protocol with those of the actors revealed two different ways of learning a script verbatim. The actors' protocols supplied converging evidence that actors have a unique strategy that puts so much effort into deriving the unstated implications of the exact words that the words themselves are retained. At no time did the actors attempt to memorize the words directly, but rather tried to discern why the character would use those particular words to express that particular thought. On those relatively rare occasions when actors addressed memorization, they discussed ease of learning due to factors within the dramatic situation, never extraneous to it. That is, the actors appeared to construct a causal chain in which every line is not only a response to the words of the cue, but a continuing investigation of what actors call a "through line" for the whole scene. This establishment of causality has frequently been shown to increase comprehension and retention (e.g., Fletcher & Bloom, 1988; Graesser & Clark, 1985; Trabasso, Secco, & van den Broek, 1984; Trabasso, van den Broek, & Liu, 1988). The mnemonist's approach was to memorize the script directly using imagery mediation; the actor's approach was to understand what mental processes of the characters' made those specific words necessary.

Gordon et al. (1984) tested a mnemonist, T. E., on a number of classical long-term and short-term memory tasks. T. E.'s basic strategy was the same as Lorayne's: converting the verbal or numerical information into images, then linking them into chains. (This is hardly surprising considering that T. E. reportedly became interested in mnemonics after reading Lorayne's book *How to Develop a Super-Power Memory*, 1957). Although Gordon et al. referred to these chains as "stories," they were not used to recall discourse verbatim. Also, a totally different type of device called the "story mnemonic" has frequently been described in the literature (e. g., Bower & Clark, 1969), but in this case the story is a framework to connect the to-be-remembered items into a memorable narrative. That is, the function of the narrative is simply to tie together a number of discrete items so that they have a connection with one another; this approach is not designed to facilitate verbatim recall of text.

One interesting aspect of Lorayne's protocol concerns the device we referred to as the miniscenario. What differentiates it from other mnemonic devices is that instead of being an image of a particular moment in time, it is more like a motion picture that evolves from one state of affairs to another, allowing Lorayne to encode the script verbatim. That is, events are added to the scenario until all the salient words have been coded (or in the case of MS2, until the scenario is sufficiently constrained so as to prompt the exact to-be-remembered words).

The difference between what we uncovered here and the mnemonic approaches to recalling prose investigated by Gruneberg (1978), Krebs et al. (1978), and Snowman et al. (1980), is that Lorayne uses the evolving images of the miniscenario to code as many words as necessary to recall text with word-for-word accuracy. The other approaches use images to retrieve the main ideas of material, which are then expressed in one's own words.

Because Lorayne has written more than 15 books (some of them best sellers), one wonders why so few actors report using his methods. They are unquestionably highly efficient. In a single demonstration, Lorayne routinely learns the names of the entire audience (often numbering in the hundreds), the exact order of all 52 cards in a shuffled deck, a description of all the items on any page of current issues of popular magazines, over 50 random items called out by the audience, and numerous other tests, all accomplished through visualization and association.

However, the use of extraneous images, no matter how effective in terms of recall, might prevent the sort of total immersion in the dramatic situation that acting requires. This may be why few actors rely heavily on mnemonic strategies. Anecdotal evidence (such as Anne Bancroft's statement mentioned earlier) suggests that actors do make use of mnemonic devices, especially when they find dialogue for which their normal learning strategy seems insufficient. For example, both Mel Brooks and Anne Bancroft used Lorayne's methods to learn the Polish lyrics to pop songs for their film, *To Be Or Not To Be* (Lorayne, 1988). This is, however, a relatively unusual assignment. In order for actors to effectively recreate living characters, they must process the material on a very deep level by examining why that character used those particular words. Since this process also results in the verbatim retention of the role, it would seem superfluous to learn the literal words by an additional strategy unless necessitated by the unusual nature of certain material.

CONCLUSION

Prior to our series of studies with actors, relatively little inquiry had been made into learning strategies that would produce verbatim retention of lengthy material. Throughout this book, we show that many actors acquire a verbatim representation of a theatrical role as a by-product of their script analysis. The Lorayne protocol adds to this body of knowledge by showing how imagery mediation could be applied to verbatim learning. However, actors would probably not make very frequent use of this device because their primary concern is with the characters' thoughts and emotions that underlie the words.

In a review paper, Herrmann (1987) pointed out that mnemonic devices tend to be task-specific. That is, the method of loci works best for serial learning, the story mnemonic for free recall, and imagery mediation for paired associate tasks. The Lorayne approach would appear useful for students who must learn poems, stories, or dramatic passages verbatim for class assignments but who do not have to consider the effects of learning strategy on performance.

From this study it appears that the strategies of the actor and the mnemonist, although directed toward different ends, do converge at the level of their underlying processes such as attention and elaboration. This is not to say that all their underlying processes are the same or receive the same emphasis. Indeed, as we see, the actors only occasionally mention visualization, the strategy that is the mnemonist's chief concern.

Many of the findings cited in this book were derived from actors' self-reports, retrospective protocols, summarizations, and think-aloud protocols. In a large number of these cases, actors referred to their preliminary segmentation of the script into individual goal-directed segments as "beats." In order to identify the benefit of this system of script analysis, we performed yet another experiment with professional actors (Noice & Noice, 1993a). The results of this experiment are the subject of chapter 9.

9

The Benefits of Script Segmentation

The theater literature describes a beat as a unit in which a single intention of the character underlies that section of text (Grote, 1985). Although beats might be as short as a single line or run for many pages, their distinguishing feature is that in each beat a character is pursuing an individual, immediate objective. As actress/author/teacher Hagen (1973) put it, "A beat begins under a given set of circumstances when an immediate objective sets in. It ends when that objective has succeeded or failed and new circumstances set in" (p. 175).

This technique of dividing a scene into beats is called "scoring," and most acting texts give examples of its application (e. g., Carey, 1995; for an excellent discussion of scoring, see Hagen, 1991, pp. 256–288). Many research questions are suggested by the actors' employment of this organizational device. Are the divisions inherent in the text itself so that most readers, regardless of their theatrical experience, would divide it at the same points, or would there be differences between actors' and students' segmentations of the same script? Is this method of organization in general use, or have many actors (especially those who have been out of school for some time) developed individual approaches that don't involve this type of organization? If this system is in general use among professional actors, can the criteria they use for segmenting a script be specified? Because each actor brings his or her life experience and prior knowledge to the work, will each divide it differently? Finally, does this type of organization simply lead to a deeper understanding of the role or does division into beats also result in better verbatim retention of the material?

To answer these questions, we asked professional actors and college students to divide a script into logical segments and title each segment (Noice & Noice, 1993a). A surprise recall task was then administered to measure the incidental learning that resulted from the participants' organization of the material.

There were 24 participants in this study: 12 professional actors and 12 undergraduate students. The actors were recruited from three different professional repertory theaters in the Midwest. (By professional we mean theatres operating under a contract with the professional actors' union, Actors' Equity Association.) The students were all enrolled in an introductory psychology class at Augustana College and received course credit for their participation. There were an equal number of males and females in each group. As usual, the test scene was from Behrman's (1952) *The Second Man*.

The actors were told to mark up the script as if they were preparing to read the scene at an audition, and, if they usually divided the script into sections, to label each one using whatever terms they would ordinarily employ. Because the students would not have any experience with this process, they were told to imagine they were going to try out for a role in a college play, and to divide the script into whatever they would consider logical segments that might help them properly interpret the scene when they read it at the tryout. Actors, by virtue of their experience, know that they do not generally perform from memory at this type of audition; however, to insure that both groups were treated equally in this respect, all participants were told that they would read the script aloud at this imaginary audition or tryout.

All participants were allowed 20 minutes to perform the task and were then given a 2-minute distractor task. This was followed by a surprise free recall test in which participants were told to write down all lines they could recall of their assigned character, verbatim if possible. During this recall phase, the experimenter took the segmented scripts into another room and copied the titles of the beats onto sheets of ruled paper. When the participants indicated they had retrieved everything they could, the experimenter collected their recall sheets and gave each one the list of his or her own beat titles. The experimenter asked the participants to read over the titles and write down any lines they had not recalled before but remembered now as a result of seeing the titles of their segments.

BEAT DIVISIONS

Analysis of the segmented scripts showed that actors created far more divisions than students, resulting in smaller beats. A summary of the number and size of beats is presented in Table 9.1. As can be seen, the size of beats ranged from 2.61 to 10.50 idea units for actors, and from 6.25 to 14.50 for students. Frequently, actors had created beats as small as 2 idea units. In some cases, actors' beats consisted of a single idea unit. However, among all beats generated by students, only one was as small as 2 idea units. Thus, in general, students created fewer but larger segments.

Beat Descriptions

One major question was whether there were qualitative differences in the participants' descriptions of the segments. To give a picture of this process,

TABLE 9.1

Number and Size of Beats Generated by Actors and Students

	Actors			Students		
	Males	Females	Mean	Males	Females	Mean
Average number of beats	9.00	7.83	8.42	4.67	4.67	4.67
Average number of idea units per beat	4.64	5.50	5.07	8.78	9.64	9.21
Average range in size from smallest to largest	2.83–9.83	2.50–11.17	2.61–10.50	4.83–13.83	7.67–15.17	6.25–14.50

Note. From "The Effects of Segmentation on the Recall of Theatrical Material," by H. Noice and T. Noice, 1993, Poetics, 22, p. 56. Copyright © 1993 by Elsevier. Adapted with permission.

a portion of the script as segmented by an actor and by a student, is presented in Fig. 9.1. As is shown, to the actor, this section consisted of two beats whereas, to the student, it consisted of one. The titles of their segments showed goal-directed activity on the part of the actor but not on the part of the student. Furthermore, both beats of the actor were from the perspective of the assigned character, whereas the student's beat was from the perspective of both characters simultaneously.

In general, two main differences in script segmentation emerged. First, actors appeared to regard each beat as an attempt by the character to achieve a particular goal and divided the script accordingly, whereas students made divisions at apparent changes in the story line, as signified by changes in topics of conversation. Second, students did not appear to adopt their assigned character's viewpoint when describing beats but either referred to both characters simultaneously (e.g., they did this; they said that) or alternated between one character's perspective and another's.

To investigate the degree of generality of these differences, all descriptions were scored along two dimensions: presence of goal-directed activity and use of perspective. Goal-directed activity was considered present if the description of the beat mentioned or strongly implied taking action toward a specific goal (e.g., "to put him at ease"). Any beat description that referred to a static situation (e.g., "Compliments are exchanged") was scored as lacking goal-directed activity. In terms of perspective, the descriptions were coded with respect to the perspective of the person performing the action. Since the experimental instructions asked the participants to study the scene as if they were auditioning (or trying out) for the same sex character, their beat descriptions were scored as "same," "different," or "both."

For example, next to a section of text in which the female character asks the male character why he rarely visits, a female participant wrote, "I want to get to know you." Clearly, the participant identified with the assigned character; therefore, the beat was scored as "same." When a male participant wrote, "Kendall shows her feelings," this utterance was scored as "different." When the description viewed both characters simultaneously (e.g., "The two made idle chit chat"), the statement was scored as "both."

All in all, 131 beat descriptions were scored, 77 generated by actors and 54 generated by students. Actually, the participants had generated a total of 157 beat descriptions (actors: 101, students: 56), but some were eliminated from the analysis because they were illegible, ambiguous, or lacked sufficient information to be categorized.

Table 9.2 presents the distribution of all the beat descriptions scored in terms of goal-directed activity and use of perspective. Independent samples t-tests were used to analyze whether there were significant differences

Actor's Description	Script	Student's Description
Share Suspicion	Kendall: (After a moment) I think you can trust Storey. Austin: Can I? Kendall: He told me over the phone—you and Miss Grey are engaged. Austin: There's something funny about it. Kendall: There's something funny about most things.	They started wondering about several things
Out with it— Trust	Austin: (Warming to her) Mrs. Frayne . . . Kendall: Call me Kendall. Austin: Thank you. I wonder—wonder if Storey tells me everything. I mean—about Monica and himself. Kendall: Perhaps he doesn't know everything. Austin: You mean—perhaps he's in love with her and doesn't know it.	

FIG. 9.1. Excerpt of the script as segmented by a male actor and a male student. *Note.* From "The Effects of Segmentation on the Recall of Theatrical Material," by H. Noice and T. Noice, 1993, *Poetics*, 4, p. 56. Copyright © 1993 by Elsevier. Reprinted with permission.

TABLE 9.2
Comparison of Beat Descriptions Generated by Actors and Students in Terms of Presence of Goal-Directed Activity and Use of Perspective

	Presence of goal-directed activity	Perspective			
		Same	Different	Both	N/S
Actors	78%**	83%**	4%	6%	8%
Students	22%	14%	33%*	50%**	3%

Note. N/S = Not specified; *p < .05; **p < .01. From "The Effects of Segmentation on the Recall of Theatrical Material," by H. Noice and T. Noice, 1993, Poetics, 22, p. 58. Copyright © 1993 by Elsevier. Adapted with permission.

between actors and students. Two findings were most important for our purposes. First, actors generated significantly more descriptions containing goal-directed activities than did students, $t(22) = 6.12, p < .01$. Second, more of the actors' descriptions reflected the perspective of the assigned character, $t(22) = 8.61, p < .01$. On the other hand, significantly more students' descriptions reflected the viewpoint of both characters, $t(22) = 5.04, p < .01$. In general, whereas actors described goal-directed activities from the viewpoint of the assigned character (e.g., "to bring her in"), students appeared to stand outside the situation and describe a static state of affairs (e.g., "Austin and Kendall discuss how honest their partners appear to be.")

Two independent raters also analyzed these descriptions along these two dimensions. Interrater agreement amounted to 94% for presence of goal statements and 97% for use of perspective. Disagreements between the raters were resolved by discussion.

Location of Beat Divisions

The next question of interest concerned the location of divisions. If both groups divided the text at the same places, it would indicate that those divisions were inherent in the text. Results showed that indeed some breaks in the narrative were so salient that both actors and students made beat divisions at that point. For example, in the following section, most participants made a division after Austin's line, "Thank you."

> Kendall: I know. Still I do wish you'd come some time—and bring Miss Grey.
> Austin: Thank you.
> Kendall: (Noticing him staring at MONICA'S colored scarf which is lying across a chair) What is it? (see Appendix A)

As is obvious, the discovery of the scarf changes the focus and introduces a switch in the topic of conversation. Although both groups were sensitive to this (75% of the actors and 92% of the students divided the script there), actors generally showed a greater tendency than students to impose their own organization on the text. For instance, in this example, 11 out of 12 actors divided the script some place prior to Austin's "Thank you," resulting in 24 beat divisions for all actors combined. However, only 7 out of 12 students divided the script prior to that point, resulting in 8 divisions for all students combined. Overall, 62% of the actors' beat divisions were made at places where only one other (or no other) actor made them, indicating an individualistic approach. Conversely, only 34.5% of the students' beats exhibited this pattern. Thus, it appears that the majority of the time, actors divided the script in places where other actors did not, whereas students divided the script in places where other students did.

Titling of Beats

Frequently, there were variations in the basic meaning actors or actresses assigned to certain sections. For example, in a certain section, one actor created three beats:

- "Ruing involvement."
- "Plea for understanding."
- "Balancing science against human values."

Analyzing the same general section, another actor entitled his beats:

- "What's the use?"
- "Maybe there's hope."
- "I give up."

Here, the actors differed in their views of the underlying meaning of these speeches. The students, on the other hand, appeared to derive less varied meanings for the same segment as suggested by such titles as:

- "Austin and Kendall wondered whether Monica and Storey were in love."
- "They are getting frustrated because they do not know the situation between Monica and Storey."
- "Austin and Kendall wonder about caring."

Even when actors or actresses appeared to agree on the basic meaning, their segmentation was far from uniform. For example, in an early section of the script, one actress created two beats:

- "Gather information and ally."
- "Butter him up/flirt."

Another actress derived four beats from approximately the same section of text:

- "To put him at ease."
- "To amuse."
- "To start conversation."
- "To flatter/to draw him out."

In these examples, the difference was mainly in degree. That is, the second actress created finer-grained beats with the same basic interpretation.

RECALL DATA

Participants' free recall protocols were analyzed to determine if segmenting the text benefitted recall. Of interest were the amount of recall and the degree of its accuracy (verbatim or paraphrased). Two different measures were used. The first, "acceptable verbatim," demanded an almost perfect word-for-word match; this measure allowed only minor deviations, such as contractions of verbs or substitutions such as "gone" for "had gone." (Chap. 4 provides a detailed description of the rules for scoring recall that is close to but not exactly verbatim.) However, of interest was also how much of the gist of the text could be recalled. Therefore, nonverbatim but meaning-preserving utterances were scored as "paraphrases" (the second measure), and any ideas not present in the original text were regarded as guesses and were not tabulated. Two independent raters scored all of the recall data. Agreements ranged from 92% for acceptable verbatim to 97% for guesses. Any disagreements were resolved by a third rater.

Table 9.3 presents a summary of the proportion of idea units correctly recalled. These data were first analyzed with a 2 x 2 between-subjects ANOVA, with expertise (actors vs. students) and assigned character (males vs. females) as the independent variables. Since males and females were assigned different roles and therefore were required to recall different lines from the script, assigned character (Kendall's vs. Austin's lines) was included as a variable. Actors recalled significantly more lines with word-for-word accuracy (or slightly changed) than did students, $F(1, 20) = 28.33$, $MSe = .006$, $p < .01$. Even when the most stringent measure of recall was used that allowed not even the slightest deviation, actors still outperformed students substantially, $F(1, 20) = 28.95$, $MSe = .002$, $p < .01$. In both analyses, the interaction between expertise and assigned character was not significant, $F < 1.0$.

TABLE 9.3
Proportion of Idea Units (of the Assigned Character) Correctly Recalled by Actors and Students

	Actors			Students		
	Males	Females	Mean	Males	Females	Mean
True verbatim	.16	.14	.15	.04	.05	.05
Acceptable verbatim	.24	.26	.25	.06	.11	.09
Paraphrase	.15	.27	.21	.15	.18	.17
Total	.39	.53	.46	.21	.29	.25

Note. Acceptable verbatim measure includes True verbatim. From "The Effects of Segmentation on the Recall of Theatrical Material," by H. Noice and T. Noice, 1993, Poetics, 22, p. 60. Copyright © 1993 by Elsevier. Adapted with permission.

To assess participants' gist recall, we compared the proportion of idea units that were paraphrased by either group. Neither the main effect of expertise nor the interaction between expertise and assigned character was significant, $F(1, 20) = 1.93$ and $F(1, 20) = 1.78, MSe = .005, p > .05$, respectively. However, females generated significantly more paraphrases than males, $F(1, 20) = 5.98, MSe = .005, p < .05$. There was no significant effect of expertise nor an expertise by assigned character interaction. Also, the two groups did not differ in terms of the number of guesses they generated. In general, guessing was minimal ($M = 2$ guesses).

The comparatively poor recall by students was not due to their failure to recall entire segments; both groups had approximately the same percentage of beats represented in their recall protocols. Students recalled one or more lines from 80% of their beats, and actors recalled one or more lines from 82% of their beats. In order to determine if these results would also hold for individual participants, a second comparison assessed how many of them had been able to recall at least one idea unit from every one of their beats. In both groups, there were six who had successfully recalled material from every one of their beats. Thus the major difference between the two groups was in terms of the number of lines recalled. That is, when actors recalled a beat, they tended to recall several speeches from that same beat whereas students frequently recalled only one.

The prompted recall task, in which participants were given the titles they had generated, produced a minor amount of additional recall for students (1.25 idea units) but almost none for actors (.17). Posttest interviews revealed that during the initial recall test, all actors had mentally gone through their beats; therefore the prompted recall was of no benefit to them.

Temporal Order

Actors must retain not only the lines of dialogue in a script but the exact order of those lines. Therefore, we next examined whether the two groups differed in their tendency to recall the dialogue in the original order. If actors and students use different approaches, does one approach result in better memory for the temporal ordering of events? If it does, this would imply that that approach may be capable of establishing connectivity between statements. To analyze the participants' ability to recall the material in its correct order, we used the seriation measure developed by Asch and Ebenholz (1962). The average index for actors was .88, significantly higher than the .65 of the students, $t(22) = 3.26$, $p < .01$, indicating that the actors had a greater tendency to recall the lines of the script in their original order.

DISCUSSION

This study set out to determine whether experienced professional actors segment a script as commonly taught in theatre training programs and, if they do, to ascertain the criteria they use and the benefits they derive from such segmentation. All actors in the study did indeed divide the script into a series of units, each one devoted to a separate intention of the assigned character. Furthermore, after segmenting the text, actors recalled three times as much material verbatim as did the students.

The question is why does this script division enhance memory in actors but not in students? Research reported in chapter 4 showed that, in the first 20 minutes of study, actors are not better memorizers per se than students; their recall is equal when both use strategies they consider appropriate to the task at hand. We believe the explanation lies in the way both groups segmented the text. The students appeared to look for natural breaks in the story where the topic of conversation suddenly changed. Although this required understanding the literal meanings of the lines, it did not require in-depth probing to discover alternate meanings not immediately apparent. However, the actors' approach called for examining each line to find out what goal the actor was pursuing when uttering those exact words. Was it the same goal the character was pursuing in the preceding line? If not, the actor started a new beat, and the in-depth processing of each utterance would have to continue in order to find the next place in the scene that called for a change in goal-directed activity. The extra attention to every line of text required by this type of analysis appears to be at least partially responsible for the actors' superior recall.

In addition to increased attention, the nature of actors' organization of a script may itself facilitate retention. Many studies have shown that information that is well organized is also better recalled (e.g., Bellezza,

Richards, & Geiselman, 1976; Mandler, 1967). One way to organize information is to sort it by category. For example, Bower, Clark, Winzenz, and Lesgold (1969) demonstrated a facilitative effect of hierarchical organization on recall.

However, organizing items into categories differs from organizing scripted scenes into beats. In the former, randomly presented groups of items are sorted according to a categorical scheme, whereas, in the latter, the order or sequence of events is fixed by the writer; a great deal of mental effort must be made by the reader in order to glean the underlying organization of dialogue that may at first glance seem like random conversation. The actors' division of each scene into goals and subgoals appeared to result in the construction of a causal chain. For example, one actress created the following sequence of beat descriptions: "To start conversation;" "To flatter and draw him out;" and "To allay any fears." In this sequence, first the female character engages the male character in conversation, then having engaged him, she flatters him and draws him out; having drawn him out, she notes that he responds fearfully and she subsequently attempts to allay that fear. The causal linkage is obvious. Her drawing him out is responsible for his revealing his fear, and this revelation is responsible for her attempt to allay that fear.

This causal chaining had a bearing on the results. Not only was there greater overall recall by actors, but also there was a greater tendency to recall lines in their original order. Students' beat descriptions did not for the most part suggest causality. For example, one student supplied the following sequence: "They are giving greetings;" "They were both giving each other friendly excuses;" and "He was curious about Monica and the scarf." The notion of causality seems to be absent. That is, the success or failure of one beat does not make the next beat necessary in the same sense that the actor's sequence does.

In addition to influencing recall, it has frequently been suggested that drawing causal inferences is a critical component of the comprehension process (e.g., Black & Bower, 1980; Graesser, 1981; Keenan, Baillet, & Brown, 1984; Long, Seely, & Oppy, 1996; Trabasso & van den Broek, 1985; van den Broek, 1990). That is, narrative text is understood in the same way as actions are in the real world: by inferring the motivations or plans behind the actions. If this causal attribution process is a general component of story comprehension, why did actors and students differ with respect to the amount of goal-directed behavior they discovered in the scene? McKoon and Ratcliff (1986; 1992) have presented evidence that under certain circumstances participants may not draw all the causal inferences necessary for complete understanding. McKoon and Ratcliff's results would seem to apply here. The students may have made only such causal inferences as were necessary to understand the overall story line. However, actors, due to their training and experience, almost always investigate the text to determine their assigned character's plan. Thus, it is not surprising that in this study actors drew many specific causal inferences that students did not.

Differences between actors' and students' approaches can be found by examining the places at which participants opted to divide the material. Consider the following section:

Kendall: (After a moment) I think you can trust Storey.
Austin: Can I?
Kendall: He told me over the phone—you and Miss Grey are engaged.
Austin: There's something funny about it.
Kendall: There's something funny about most things.
Austin: (Warming to her) Mrs. Frayne...

In the above excerpt, all of the male actors and none of the male students segmented the script after the line, "There's something funny about most things." The data indicated that the actors, but not the students, tended to identify with their assigned characters. Therefore, if an actor was looking at that section of the scene from the male character's perspective, his beat descriptions should suggest that Austin (before saying, "Mrs. Frayne...") makes a decision to put his trust in Kendall. This indeed was the case with the actors, as indicated by their descriptive titles for that segment (e.g., "Exploring trust of Storey more directly with Kendall," "Bring her in," "Pull her into your suspicion," "Out with it—trust").

On the other hand, none of the male students divided the scene at that line, apparently regarding the entire stretch of dialogue as one segment. This is shown by their use of such titles as, "Austin and Kendall suspect their lovers may have fallen in love with each other," "They started wondering about several things," "Austin reflects on his dinner with Monica," "Austin doesn't trust Storey." Even though some of these students' descriptions are made from Austin's viewpoint, they nevertheless do not explore his ongoing mental activity, but simply summarize what is being discussed in that section.

Thus, the differences in use and specificity of perspective appear to be responsible for the decision to segment at a particular spot. The actors had identified with Austin so completely they took on his moment-to-moment thought processes, and this identification resulted in all of the actors starting a new beat after the line, "There's something funny about most things." This perspective taking also appears to help explain the actors' superior recall results. As Trabasso and van den Broek (1985) pointed out, "specifically, events that are best recalled ... describe the consequences of the protagonist's goal-directed action" (p. 612). By identifying so closely with their assigned characters, actors necessarily think of those characters as the protagonists in that particular situation.

Although actors frequently agreed about the underlying meaning of a section, they did not always do so. For example, one actor appeared to regard a group of lines as representing an attempt by the character to enlist the other character's help. Another actor considered that same general section of text as representing an attempt by that character to woo the other character. Thus, actors' beat divisions might be considered as one of their creative contributions to the eventual performance. Each actor's interpretation of the script, as indicated by his or her individual beat divisions, affects the actor's vocal inflections, facial expressions, and body language.

CONCLUSION

This experiment brings us one step closer to an understanding of actors' mental processes. In chapter 3, we showed that actors indulge in fine-grained examination of the text to determine the plans of the assigned characters. As seen in chapters 6 and 7, this examination consists of attending to both the content and the form of the text in order to determine the mental and emotional states of the characters, and to ascertain how these qualities would be made clear to an audience. This chapter examines the contributions made by the actors' methods of breaking down the text into segments. It should be emphasized that this picture of actors' mental processes is derived primarily from their first 20 minutes of contact with the script, but the results are consistent with actors' self-reports of their complete learning processes.

Up to this point, we have been summarizing the findings of our 8-year program of research. Before proposing an actors' model based on those findings, we present, in the next chapter, the results of three new studies that have yet to be reported in the cognitive literature.

10

Continuing the Quest

EXPERIMENT ONE: TEACHING THE TECHNIQUE

Because one of the purposes of expertise research is to provide information that might accelerate the transition from novice to expert, we recently performed an experiment (Noice, 1995) that investigated whether beginning actors can benefit (in terms of increased retention of material) from instruction in the learning procedures of professional actors. As pointed out in previous chapters, one of the most important aspects of a professional actor's role preparation consists of his or her organization of the script hierarchically, so that each utterance is thought of as an attempt by that character to achieve a particular goal. There is voluminous evidence in the cognitive literature to show that, in general, narrative statements that are thought of as components in a plan or steps to reach a goal are more memorable than statements not so conceived (for a discussion, see chap. 9). However, it is a characteristic of most theatrical scripts that this goal-directed structure is not immediately obvious. Plays that appear heavy-handed rarely win favor with the public, so professional playwrights proceed more by implication and suggestion than by exhortation and declaration.

It was the premise of this experiment that if acting students were presented with scripts in which the implied goals of the characters were made explicit, the exact wording of these scripts would be more memorable than if participants studied the same scripts where the goals remained merely implied. Therefore, some participants were given annotated scripts in which the scene was organized into beats, each devoted to a separate explicit goal, whereas other participants were given scripts not so annotated. Participants in the latter group had only to understand the script in sufficient depth to render the statements coherent, but students who received the annotated text were forced to indulge in a problem-solving process in order to generate a causal connection between the literal meaning of each particular line and how it constituted an attempt to reach the stated goal.

Furthermore, because each goal is generally pursued in terms of another character, another area of interest was whether visualization of a specific person during script study would benefit the learner. That is, would mentally trying obtain a goal from some unspecified person be less effective (in terms of the depth of processing that would enhance memory) than trying to obtain the same goal from a specific, visualized person? Therefore, a third group of acting students was given annotated scripts with additional instructions regarding visualization. It was predicted that recall would be greater for those participants receiving annotated scripts than for those receiving nonannotated ones, and that there would be additional recall generated by the visualization procedure.

Design and Procedure

Eighteen students in a beginning acting class participated as a course requirement. The materials consisted of a two-person scene between a character named Joe and another named Mary from the William Saroyan play *Time of Your Life* (1939). The scene takes place in a bar where Joe strikes up a conversation with Mary while she is waiting for her husband. The criteria for choosing this scene were the same as for our other test scene from *The Second Man*. Participants were randomly assigned to one of three conditions:

Training Condition. Scripts contained not only the author's original dialogue and stage directions but also had additions in the margins describing the character's underlying intention for each group of lines, as previously determined by a professional actor. (A page of the annotated script can be found in Appendix C.)

Training Plus Visualization. Scripts were annotated in the same way but contained additional instructions regarding the visualization of a scene partner.

Memorization (Control) Condition. Scripts contained only the author's original dialogue and stage directions. Each group was tested separately. All participants were given booklets containing the script. In the experimental conditions, female participants were told to *imagine* they would be playing the role of Mary and male participants were told to *imagine* they would be playing the role of Joe. In the control condition, male participants were told to *memorize* the role of Joe and female participants the role of Mary.

Participants in the training condition were instructed to read silently through the script once to see what it was about and then to go back to the beginning, think about the handwritten beat descriptions of the character's intentions in the margins, then read the assigned character's lines while trying actively to achieve the stated intentions in their imaginations. Furthermore, they were told to repeat each section three times before going on to the next. On each repetition, they were to speak their own character's lines aloud and to read the other character's silently. After completing the script in this manner, they were told that if they had any time left they should start again at the beginning. These participants were told specifically not to try to memorize the words, but that later there would be a test to see how many of the words "stuck in their heads" as a result of actively using the intentions.

Participants in the training plus visualization condition received the identical materials and instructions, but in addition were told to visualize (as the other character in the scene) someone whose face they could recall easily and that when speaking the words of the script aloud, they should imagine they were trying to affect the person they were visualizing.

Participants in the memorization (control) condition were told to use whatever strategy they generally used when learning materials that had to be recalled verbatim. All participants studied their scripts for 12 minutes and then performed a brief interpolated task. They then received recall scripts in which only the other character's lines appeared. No time limit was given for filling in the assigned characters' lines, but all participants completed the task within 20 minutes.

Scoring

The entire script had been segmented into idea units (55 for Joe and 43 for Mary), as agreed on by two raters. As in previous experiments, accuracy was assessed along three dimensions: "verbatim," "almost verbatim," and "paraphrased." The scoring rules were almost identical to those described in chapter 3.

Reliability of Scoring. After one training session with materials from another play, two independent raters scored all of the recall protocols. There was 99.7% agreement for true verbatim, 96.4% for almost verbatim, and 83% for paraphrase. Any disagreements were resolved by a third independent rater.

RECALL PERFORMANCE

True Verbatim Recall

For all analyses the rejection level was set at .05. Of primary interest was how much of the text was recalled with word-for-word accuracy. The results are shown in Table 10.1. As can be seen, after only 12 minutes of study, participants in the training plus visualization condition recalled 57% of the script verbatim, compared to 25% for controls. A two-factor (condition and assigned character) between-subjects analysis of variance (ANOVA) produced one significant effect, that of condition, $F(2, 12) = 6.87, MSe = .023$. A follow-up analysis using a Tukey post hoc test indicated that training plus visualization resulted in significantly greater verbatim recall relative to the memorization condition. Because the recall of males and females did not

TABLE 10.1
Means and Standard Deviations for True Verbatim Recall as a Function of Learning Task

	Learning Instruction		
	Training Plus Visualization	Training	Memorization (Control)
Males	.497 (.074)	.343 (.150)	.248 (.227)
Females	.643 (.075)	.589 (.075)	.248 (.132)
Mean	.570	.466	.248

differ significantly ($F < 1$), nor interact with condition, $F(1, 12) = 1.87$, the analyses that follow were collapsed over the gender variable.

Almost Verbatim

Of additional interest was how much of the text would be remembered when assessed by a slightly more lenient measure (almost verbatim) that allowed minor, precisely specified changes. When this additional recall was added to true verbatim recall, the resulting measure, nearly verbatim, represented the total that a participant remembered word for word or almost word for word. A one-way, between-subjects ANOVA performed on this dependent variable indicated that the three groups differed significantly, $F(2, 15) = 10.95$, $MSe = .026$. A Tukey post hoc analysis revealed that participants who had received either of the two training instructions remembered more of the playscript verbatim or nearly verbatim ($M = 66\%$, $M = 72.7\%$ respectively) than participants who had received memorization instructions ($M = 31.7\%$).

Paraphrases

To assess whether any of the three study strategies tended to result in recall of the overall ideas rather than the exact wording, an additional analysis of variance (ANOVA) was performed on paraphrased lines only. This produced a significant effect, $F(2, 15) = 6.01$, $MSe = .003$. A Tukey post hoc test showed a recall advantage for paraphrased lines only for both of the training conditions ($M = 18\%$ and $M = 17\%$) compared to the memorization condition ($M = 7\%$).

Total Recall

Finally, overall recall was assessed (nearly verbatim plus paraphrases). A one-way analysis of variance (ANOVA) indicated that participants differed significantly in terms of their overall recall, $F(2, 15) = 17.71$, $MSe = .024$.

Post hoc tests showed participants in both the training and training-plus-visualization conditions remembered more of the playscript (M = 83% and M = 90%) than those in the memorization condition (M = 41%). The results for all recall conditions are shown in Table 10.2.

DISCUSSION

This study set out to investigate whether students in a beginning acting class would receive the same memory boost that experienced actors do if they were instructed in the use of experienced actors' memory strategies. The results showed that, at all levels of accuracy (from verbatim to paraphrase), participants who studied the lines of the script as if they were attempts by the characters to achieve specific goals, retained significantly more material than did controls who were simply told to memorize the material. These results appeared to supply additional evidence that the facility with which professional actors learn material is at least partially dependent on the elaborative memory processes brought into play by the nature of their script learning strategies. The processes would appear to be additive. That is, when imagery was added to the establishment of causality, overall verbatim recall increased. However, when the slightly more lenient measure (nearly verbatim) was used, although both experimental groups outperformed controls, there was no significant difference between the groups with and without visualization instructions. This pattern of results is puzzling. Why should imagery have an additive effect for exact verbatim recall but not for recall that was nearly, but not exactly, verbatim?

One explanation might be that even without visualization, the organization of the playscript into beats benefits retention. That is, by being required to relate a specific line to an overall goal, students necessarily engaged in

TABLE 10.2

Mean Proportion of Idea Units Recalled for All Recall Measures

	Learning Instruction		
	Training Plus Visualization	Training	Memorization (Control)
True verbatim	.570 (.104)	.466 (.171)	.248 (.166)
Almost verbatim	.156 (.059)	.194 (.062)	.069 (.058)
Acceptable verbatim*	.726 (.140)	.660 (.178)	.317 (.168)
Paraphrase	.178 (.045)	.169 (.056)	.074 (.069)
Total	.904 (.079)	.830 (.173)	.391 (.187)

Note. Acceptable verbatim consists of True verbatim and Almost verbatim.

relational processing. In order to do this, they had to attend to the specific words, which also resulted in item-specific processing (see Einstein & Hunt, 1980; and McDaniel & Einstein, 1989, for a discussion of these topics). In other words, the nature of our stimuli specified the characters' goals, and, as a result, the participants had to extract the causal relationships by elaborating on the dialogue to determine why the character used those specific words to achieve those specific intentions.

Why did participants who also had to visualize the person to whom they were saying those words tend to remember them with even greater precision? One explanation might be that when a participant must use certain words to affect a particular person in his or her imagination, the participant is forced to consider whether those exact words would be effective with respect to that particular person. For example, at one point in the script, Mary asks Joe, "Do you always drink a great deal?" If the participant had visualized as Joe a person she knew always drank a great deal, the exact words would be memorable because of their appropriateness. Conversely, if the participant were picturing a person known to be a teetotaler, the words might be memorable because of their incongruity. If the participant were visualizing a person whose drinking habits were unknown, she would be forced to consider just how applicable the words were. In any case, the visualization of a specific person as Joe would require the participant to give extra consideration to the appropriateness of the line, "Do you always drink a great deal?"

The results of this experiment add to the already extensive evidence that the assigning of causal relationships facilitates memory. Of course, in a real-world situation, the actors would not receive an annotated script but would have to do the analyzing themselves. The extra effort involved in generating these analyses (and the resulting arousal) would no doubt make the procedure even more efficacious. (For a discussion of self-generated as opposed to experimenter-supplied answers, see chap. 3; see also Begg, Vinski, Frankovich, & Holgate, 1991; Jacoby, 1978; Kahneman, 1973.)

This experiment shows that even beginning acting students benefit when the experimental task brings certain cognitive learning principles into play. This raises a question: Was the facilitation observed with beginning actors solely a result of the experimental manipulation or was some of it due to the students' motivation? Most acting students possess an intense desire to improve their skills. The question is, "Would the strategy be equally beneficial to less highly motivated students?" To answer this, we are currently replicating the experiment with psychology students who have no professed interest in acting. Still another question concerns the possibility that the relatively high recall by the two experimental groups might have been partially due to the active way they were instructed to perform the task: speaking aloud and trying hard to obtain the goals in their imaginations.

The contribution of active experiencing to recall is also a subject of current investigation.

EXPERIMENT TWO: THE END OF THE PROCESS

Thus far, the experiments we described have concentrated on the encoding strategies of actors. Recently our colleague, Arnold Glass, pointed out that Tulving (1983) had proposed an experiment in which participants would memorize a short story from classical literature (e. g., Sir Walter Scott's "The Two Drovers") and would subsequently be given recognition and recall tasks for selected words that the participants presumably would have been exposed to only in the context of that story (e. g., *poniard*). Tulving and his associates (Tulving, 1984; Tulving & Thomson, 1973; Tulving & Watkins, 1977; Tulving & Wiseman, 1975; Watkins & Tulving, 1975) have shown recognition failure of recallable words in a variety of circumstances and have suggested that this phenomenon is evidence that episodic memory is functionally different from semantic memory. In his Presidential Address at the meeting of the American Psychological Association, Tulving (1985) revised his semantic–episodic distinction by proposing a monohierarchical classification. In his revised scheme, memory is viewed as a ternary system with episodic memory embedded in semantic memory (see Tulving, 1985 for a complete description; see also, McKoon, Ratcliff, & Dell, 1986 for a critique of this distinction).

If, in the experiment proposed by Tulving, participants failed to recognize as "old" such words as *poniard* but could produce them when given the original learning context, this would extend the phenomenon of recognition failure of recallable words to well-learned material. When he proposed that experiment, Tulving referred to a similar one executed some years before by Lachman and Field (1965), who taught participants 50-word prose passages, word for word, and subsequently had them perform recall and recognition tasks. Results showed that even though the participants could recite the passages perfectly, they were only about 80% successful in recognizing the 50 target words on a list of 100 words. Tulving (1983) pointed out that Lachman and Field's methodology was criticized because participants were given only 1.5 seconds to accept or reject a word on the recognition task. Therefore, he suggested "The Two Drovers" experiment in which participants would be taught a short story containing some unusual words and then perform a recognition task and a fill-in-the-blank task for the unusual words.

It seems that this experiment was never performed, probably due to the problem of recruiting participants who are willing and able to memorize a story of approximately 8,000 words verbatim. (Lachman & Field took as many as 128 sessions spread over 4 days to teach their participants 50-word prose passages.) Because our ongoing investigation of professional actors' expertise puts us in contact with subjects who routinely memorize lengthy material verbatim, we designed an experiment along the lines of the one Tulving proposed, using Shakespearean roles previously memorized and performed by our participants (Noice & Noice, 1996c). However, our primary purpose was not to test episodic–semantic distinctions. Most of our previous research on professional acting expertise concentrated on encoding strategies; this experiment would allow us to investigate the end result of the process by determining the degree to which, in the absence of any contextual cues, actors could recognize words from roles they had not performed for some months. This is, to us, highly relevant to an understanding of acting expertise. If, as many actors claim, they think on stage as the character would in that situation, then it stands to reason that the words must come from the character's lexicon. Obviously the character would not be repeating a memorized speech but choosing words that suit the needs of the ongoing situation. If actors can reliably distinguish single words of a script from foils in the absence of any contextual cues whatsoever, it would imply that each individual word has entered the actor's lexicon and is no longer simply part of the memorized chain of dialogue.

Design and Procedure

The participants were eight professional actors who had not performed the roles from which the stimuli were generated for at least 3 months and had learned two or three new roles in the interim. They were given a word list consisting of 10 unusual Shakespearean words, 20 low frequency words (Kucera & Francis, 1967), and 10 pseudowords. (A large list of potential pseudowords was pretested with different participants, and only those pseudowords that were mistaken for real words 50% of the time were used.) The low frequency words and pseudowords were the same for every participant, but the Shakespearean words were selected from roles each individual actor had played in the past. The Shakespearean words were all unusual (e.g., extirp, enskied, oisser) and probably would not have ever been encountered even by actors except in the course of playing the particular role from which they were drawn. (All such words were either from *Measure for Measure* or *Romeo and Juliet*.) Due to their extremely long original running times (often as much as 4 hours), few Shakespearean plays are performed intact. Therefore, in addition to locating the target words in the original script, it was necessary to view video tapes of the productions in question to make sure all participants had actually used the target words in their performances.

The stimuli in the word lists were arranged in random order. However, the following constraints were observed:

1. No two Shakespearean words were allowed to appear in a row.
2. The first Shakespearean word could not appear earlier than the fifth position on the list.
3. Shakespearean words had to be separated by at least one real word (i.e., two Shakespearean words could not be separated solely by a pseudoword).

Word lists were constructed for each of the eight participants. Therefore, all in all, there were 80 Shakespearean targets.

In addition to the these stimuli, individualized fill-in-the-blank passages for all target words were prepared for the participants, each passage containing one of the Shakespearean words from that actor's list. In almost every case, the contextual material was less extensive than the example given by Tulving. For instance, the following is a typical example of our fill-in-the-blank stimuli:

> I hold you as a thing _____ and sainted
> By your renouncement, an immortal spirit.

In comparison, Tulving (1983) suggested:

> Harry Wakefield fell and expired with a single groan.
> His assassin next seized the bailiff by the collar,
> and offered the bloody _____ to his throat,
> while dread and surprise rendered the man incapable of defense. (p. 269)

As can be seen, not only is the latter over twice as long, the target word is preceded by the bulk of the passage to provide ample lead-in information. Conversely, in the majority of our stimuli, the blank for the target word appeared in the first line.

Actors were first given the list of letter strings and told to write down, next to each string, a "Y" if they recognized it as a word and an "N" if they did not. If they did recognize the string as a word, they were asked to rate their degree of certainty on a 5-point scale (5 = "absolutely sure"; 1 = "not at all sure").

After completion, the actors performed the fill-in-the blank task and, subsequently, were asked to state if and when they were aware that some of the stimuli were words from Shakespearean roles they had played.

Results

Of primary interest was whether the actors could reliably identify the Shakespearean words as words in other than their original learning context. It was obvious from the beginning of the scoring that they could. With the exception of one word (out of 78), all targets were recognized. Two of the

Shakespearean words had to be eliminated from the analysis due to experimenter errors in the preparation of the stimuli. Even though the experimenters had checked the video tapes to make sure the target words had indeed been used in performance, there were two oversights. These were due to the fact that excisions in most Shakespearean plays are made by cutting entire speeches or scenes; therefore, when the experimenters went through the approximately 5 hours of video material, they checked mainly beginnings and endings of speeches. However, occasionally a director leaves a long speech intact and removes a single line or two from its middle. This was the case with the two words the actors did not recognize or recall. Rechecking the tape revealed that indeed these two words were not in the performed versions, reducing the pool of Shakespearean words to 78.

Correct Identification. Although the question of whether actors could also distinguish genuine words was of relatively minor interest (after all, they are quite a literate population), nevertheless, the proportion of Shakespearean targets, pseudowords, and words correctly identified by each participant was calculated. Means and standard deviations are shown in Table 10.3. The most important finding was the remarkable recognition of Shakespearean words (77 out of 78), indicating almost perfect discrimination between targets and lures. Participants also exhibited excellent ability to distinguish words from pseudowords ($M = .745$ for words and $M = .788$ for pseudowords). A one-way analysis of variance (ANOVA) produced a significant effect of stimulus type, $F(7, 2) = 4.844$, $MSe = .026$, $p < .05$. A post hoc multiple comparison test, using the Newman Keuls test, indicated that participants identified Shakespearean targets better than words or pseudowords.

However, for our purposes, this three-way comparison was not of primary interest. Our two main concerns were: the degree of accuracy for Shakespearean words versus the degree of accuracy for all other stimuli, and the degree of confidence regarding Shakespearean words compared to other stimuli. In the case of the former, analysis showed the average error rate was 1.25% for Shakespearean words versus 22.5% for all other stimuli.

A separate analysis was performed on the confidence ratings. Results indicated that (on a 5-point scale) participants exhibited higher confidence

TABLE 10.3

Accuracy (Percentage Correct) for the Lexical Decision Task

Shakespearean Words	Words	Pseudowords
98.63 (3.89)	75.00 (21.88)	80.00 (14.14)

in judging Shakespearean targets as words (M = 4.84) than in judging other low frequency words as words (M = 4.36), $t(7) = 4.26$, $p < .01$.

Fill-in-the-Blank Task. With the exception of the two target words that had been eliminated from the analysis, all actors completed the fill-in-the blank task with 100% accuracy. The two experimenter errors in the preparation of the stimuli allowed for some interesting inferences as to the nature of the actors' mental representations of the script. In the case of one actor, he identified the target word as a nonword and left it blank in the fill-in-the-blank task. At the end of the session, he informed the experimenter that all but one of the speeches in the second task were from a role he had played but that he was positive he had not performed the remaining speech. (He was correct, of course, because that speech was not in the performed version.) This indicated that the actor's mental representation was such that he could be certain not only of which lines were in his role but of which were not.

The second actor gave the Shakespearean word a medium confidence rating of 3 on the recognition task and did not complete the item in the fill-in-the-blank task. It turned out that the line containing the target word was in the original rehearsal script and was used during the actors' first read-through at the start of the rehearsal period. Then the director decided to cut the line so that, in point of fact, the actor had seen the target word months before the testing and indeed recognized it as a word, but not with the same confidence as the words he had actually spoken in rehearsal and performance.

As already pointed out, these two cases were not subject errors, but experimenter errors; therefore, actors' actual performance on the target words was 98.72% on the recognition task and 100% on the fill-in-the-blank task. On the follow-up question, all actors verified that they immediately realized there were Shakespearean words among the stimuli when they encountered the first one on the list.

Discussion

Tulving (1983) suggested that recognition failure of recallable words might occur with lengthy, well-learned material and proposed an experiment similar to the one described here. Our results indicated that recognition failure did not take place with roles that had been memorized verbatim, but rather that actors could reliably distinguish between target words and foils in a lexical decision task.

However, actors have described their process as similar to getting into a character's head, or getting to think like the character, or adopting that character's mind-set. As shown by the protocol statements quoted throughout this book, actors accomplish this by understanding not only the meanings of the words the characters use, but also by considering the level of education and culture those words indicate; whether they are specific to certain occupations or professions; what biases they reveal; the emotional thrust behind them and many other factors. It is not surprising, therefore, that actors could recognize the target words in other than their original contexts. Obviously, the *character* would know these words and use them in whatever context seemed appropriate, and the actor's job is to recreate, as much as possible, the totality of a character's mental and emotional life. This process appears to amplify, to a high degree, the notion of a microworld that many theorists consider to be a prime component in the understanding of narrative, (e.g., Bower, 1989; Glenberg, Meyer, & Lindem, 1987; Johnson-Laird, 1983; Zwaan, Langston, & Graesser, 1995).

The results of the fill-in-the-blank task showed the effect of encoding specificity; the context reliably cued the target words. However, the targets were equally well recognized outside the original learning context. Tulving, when he suggested this type of experiment, may have felt that there was a possibility of obtaining recognition failure for recallable words with material that had been learned by studying it over and over until retention was perfect. However, our procedure was designed to investigate acting expertise and may have been insensitive to the very issue that interested Tulving.

The theoretical point that emerges from our results is that, because of the deep processing engaged in by professional actors, the lines they learn can be recalled when they are given minimal contextual information and can be recognized without any contextual information whatsoever. In order to determine the latter, it was necessary to use a lexical decision task because that paradigm would not even hint to the actors that the task concerned Shakespearean plays or, for that matter, any type of dramatic material.

The results of this experiment extend our knowledge of professional acting expertise by showing that actors have the ability to access individual words from roles, in or out of context. The fact that 100% of our participants could do so with virtually complete accuracy suggests a high degree of generalizability for this special population. Because our version of the experiment was not designed to test the question that prompted Tulving to propose a similar one, Tulving recently suggested that we use our professional population to address this issue by having them perform a true recognition task rather than a lexical decision task. He recommended that we use fairly unusual, but not exceedingly unusual, words from a Shakespearean role, plus an equivalent number of words (of the same frequency) not in that role. The actors' task would be to accept or reject each word as coming from a particular role. If significantly more words were to be recalled in a subsequent fill-in-the-blank task than in the recognition task, it would suggest that, at some level, there was functional separability between semantic and episodic memory as proposed by Tulving. We are currently performing this experiment.

A comment frequently heard about actors' performances concerns the accuracy with which they render roles. Indeed, it has often been opined that actors take liberties with the text by doing a fair amount of ad libbing or improvising. Although this is true at times in film and television, stage actors are prohibited by contract from changing lines without the author's permission. However, to date there has been no experimental investigation of just how closely stage actors adhere to this rule.

EXPERIMENT THREE: THE QUESTION OF ACCURACY

Throughout this book, we have referred to the accuracy with which actors render playscripts. In an experiment primarily designed to address accessibility of text, Oliver and Ericsson (1986) reported that actors' recall was very exact, but they gave no statistical measures. Furthermore, the performance in the Oliver and Ericsson study was of a Shakespearean verse play where constraints of meter, rhythm, and rhyme make paraphrasing unlikely. What about other types of plays? Do the actors take liberties with the wording, making spontaneous substitutions during a performance? If so, are individual actors consistent in this regard (i.e., are some actors more prone to paraphrasing than others?)?

This has been a difficult area to research, because it is illegal to use recording devices of any sort in professional theaters. Fortunately, we have been able to obtain archival video tapes from a large regional theater for our experiments. The authors recently supervised a study (Milner & Danielson, 1995) in which the performances of two actors, each performing two different plays in the same season (one classical verse play and one contemporary farce), and two other actors performing in a social drama, were checked against copies of the original written scripts by two independent raters.

Accuracy of performance was assessed by computing the total number of words correctly recalled by each actor for each scene. These data are shown in Table 10.4. As can be seen, the actors' renditions were extremely accurate overall, and almost flawless in the case of classical verse.

Moreover, because plays develop from idea to idea rather than from word to word, the correspondence between script and performance was also analyzed in idea units. These results are shown in Table 10.5. Once again, rendition of the verse play was almost perfect, but the actors took some liberties in the drama and the farce.

A third measure concerned the types of changes that were made. The most frequent were in the form of substitutions such as, may for might, upset

TABLE 10.4
Degree of Word-for-Word Match Between Written Script and Live Performance for Three Different Scenes

	Verse		Drama		Farce	
	Female	Male	Female	Male	Female	Male
Total number of words	252	224	194	379	208	381
Total number of words missing	1	5	2	5	34	46
Accuracy	99.60%	97.77%	98.97%	98.68%	83.65%	87.93%

TABLE 10.5
Types of Changes Between Written Script and Performance (in Idea Units)

	Verse		Drama		Farce	
	Female	Male	Female	Male	Female	Male
Verbatim	39	24	29	69	19	37
	97.50%	77.42%	85.30%	97.18%	45.24%	53.62%
1–2 word changes	1	7	5	1	16	23
	2.50%	22.58%	14.70%	1.41%	38.10%	33.33%
More than 2 word changes	0	0	0	1	3	5
	0%	0%	0%	1.41%	7.14%	7.25%
Paraphrase	0	0	0	0	4	4
	0%	0%	0%	0%	9.52%	5.80%

for hurt, and talk for speak. The next most frequent type of change consisted of minor additions, such as adding the terminal word *dear* in a speech like "I think that would be lovely, *dear*." The least frequent type of change consisted of deleting words that did not materially affect meaning (e.g., deleting Oh from a speech like, "Oh, I don't know if that's really true.")

This study indicated that the degree of accuracy varied with the type of script. A classical verse play obviously places more constraints on the type of substitutions that are acceptable and therefore demands greater fidelity than a prose drama. Moreover, a farce emphasizes physical comedy, and a minor amount of verbal improvisation might be necessary to cover unforseen changes in timing or position that might result from frenetic action. Because substitutions, additions and deletions were primarily made with words such as *oh, no,* or *please,* the original meaning of the text was consistently preserved. All in all, most changes appeared to be attempts by the actors to make the text more speechlike. An additional finding was that there was no indication that some actors have a greater tendency to paraphrase than others.

Each study described in this book was performed to answer specific questions regarding the mental processes of professional actors. It is time now to use our results to propose a tentative model of acting cognition. Chapter 11 is devoted to the presentation of such a model.

11

A General Model of Acting Cognition

The following model represents the process of actually working on a given segment of a role from the first attempt to learn the text to the eventual performance. However, as indicated by the self-reports of actors (chap. 2), before scene-by-scene learning comes into play, a great deal of analytical work on the script as a whole has taken place. The preliminary analysis includes exploring the play's genre, style, era, mode of presentation and probable backgrounds of the characters. This model represents the process by which the actor commits any particular section of the script to memory after the preliminary analysis has been concluded. It should be emphasized that, in many cases, the steps would combine and/or coexist.

1. Every scene in which that actor appears (i. e., from the time the character enters till he or she leaves) is broken down into "beats," each devoted to a subgoal that must be dealt with before the scene goal can be realized.

2. The actor analyzes the individual lines that comprise each "beat," asking:

- What do the exact words tell him or her about the character and the tactics that character is using to obtain the goal in this segment?
- How does the resolution of each segment lead into the next one?

3. The actor isolates one particular segment and asks:

- What does the character want in this "beat"?
- From whom does he or she try to get it?
- What are his or her tactics?
- What must he or she overcome?
- Does he or she succeed or fail?

4. Once the actor has determined the character's goals and tactics in that segment, the actor then becomes that character in his or her imagina-

A General Model of Acting Cognition 115

tion and actively uses the words of the script to try to obtain the goal from the other person or persons in the scene. That is, the actor reads the literal words *tactically* to obtain the goals determined in Step 3.

5. The prior steps are repeated for each segment of the script, with each one then being dovetailed with the preceding and following segments. This active use of plan implementation continues rehearsal after rehearsal, gradually resulting in the retention of the exact words. When this is accomplished, the actor is said to be "off book."

6. Frequently the actor/character spontaneously changes tactics during rehearsal because the new tactics seem more appropriate for obtaining the desired goal at the moment. This spontaneous fine tuning continues for much of the rehearsal period until the performance starts to jell. Even after this period, the interpretation is never "fixed," but is kept fluid within the give and take of the various characters.

7. This active engagement in the ongoing dramatic situation gives rise to a wide variety of affect states (feelings, moods, emotions) that may vary from rehearsal to rehearsal and from performance to performance. Of

TABLE 11.1

A Model of Actors' Script-Learning Processes

Activity	Purpose
After analyzing script to determine style, era, and so forth, the actor focuses on an individual scene in which his or her character appears and breaks the scene down into individual segments called beats. (Step 1)	To determine overall goal of character during that scene and how each beat involves an attempt to obtain that overall goal.
Actor works on each individual beat. (Steps 2 and 3)	To determine how and why the character's dialogue and actions constitute attempts to obtain the beat goal.
Actor tactically uses the words to obtain the goal. This is a very active process done in the actor's imagination during individual study sessions and in conjunction with the other actors during rehearsals. (Step 4)	To identify with the character so there's no separation between actor and character. This is often referred to as "becoming" the character.
Steps 1 through 4 continue for the entire rehearsal period, working on each scene in turn before blending the scenes into run-throughs of the entire play. (Step 5)	To deepen the process of "becoming" the character, gradually absorbing the dialogue rather than rote-memorizing it.
Throughout the rehearsals and the subsequent performances, the actor continuously adjusts his or her performance based on "give-and-take" with the other actors. (Step 6)	To keep the performance "alive," so that it is spontaneous every night and not just a mechanical repetition of the preceding performance.
The affect states (Step 7) are generally most pronounced at this final stage, but can arise spontaneously during any phase.	

course, these affect states would probably appear in many of the earlier steps as well, although possibly in a less pronounced form.

This model is derived from disparate pieces of evidence, based on the many experiments reported in this book. For instance, Points 1, 2, and 3 are based largely on material reported in chapters 3, 4, and 8, whereas Points 4, 5, and 6 depend more on material reported in chapters 6 and 7, as well as material from chapters 3 and 8. Furthermore, the entire model is consistent with the analysis of the theater literature reported in chapter 2. Therefore, Table 11.1 represents one possible and, we believe, fairly typical procedure.

Table 11.1 described the course of role learning over time; we now present a hypothetical, single moment during any given performance. This interactive model is shown in Fig. 11.1. As we see, the goal-directed beat lies at the heart of the model. The text is given a specific intention by the goal, and this intention then governs the performance.

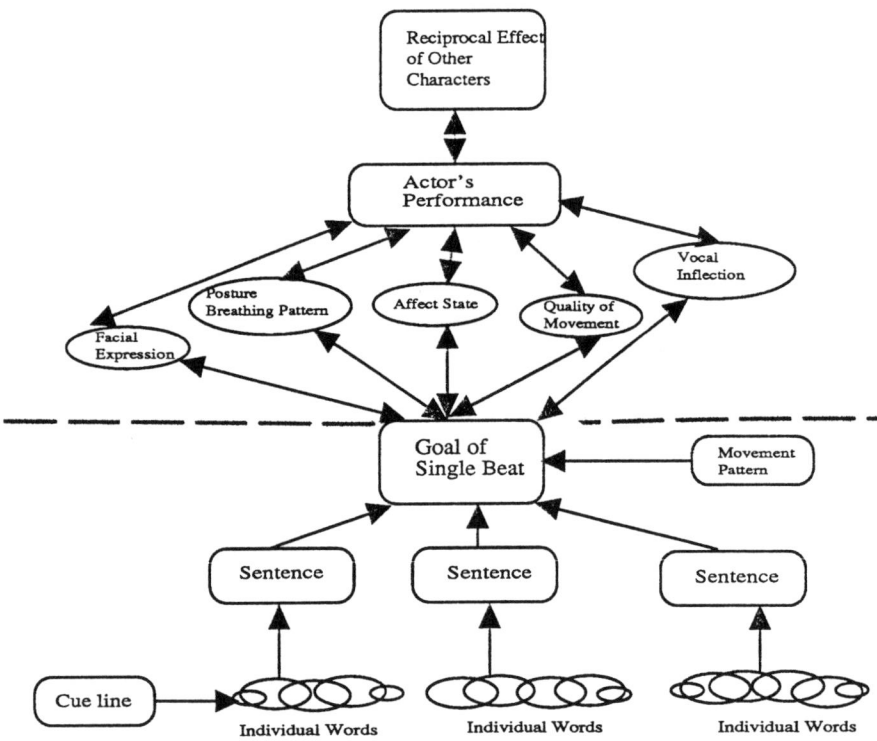

FIG. 11.1. Flow of information during an actor's performance. *Note.* The components below the dotted line constitute input from memory.

To show how the flow chart might be instantiated at any given moment of a performance, we use an example from the protocol of T. D. (This participant's entire protocol can be found in Appendix B.) The literal passage from the playscript was as follows:

> Austin: It's rotten to be this way. Wondering about everything, suspecting everybody. Why should I care if Monica came back here or not? And yet—I do. (See Appendix A)

T. D. speculated that Austin used these words to reveal his doubts to Kendall, in the hope that she would level with him.

In terms of Fig. 11.1, this passage, and any accompanying movements, comprise the input, and thus occupy the bottom level of the model. This input then feeds into the deep meaning of the "beat" (i.e., Austin reveals his own doubts in order to encourage Kendall to reveal what she knows). As a result, the words of the text become an attempt to fulfill the goal of that beat. Therefore, the goal influences the various parameters of the actor's rendition (vocal inflections, facial expressions, etc.), resulting in that particular moment of performance. However, the effect of speaking the dialogue aloud also feeds back to the goal node, subtly reinforcing or modifying the attempt to reach the goal. At the same time, the actor is aware of the effect of the dialogue on the other character, creating another feedback loop between the two characters, further conditioning the performance.

Of course, the protocol from which this example was derived was generated during the participant's first pass-through of the script. Subsequent analysis of that beat during the rehearsal period might alter T. D.'s original decision about the goal (or reconfirm it). Nevertheless, the process of applying the information at the moment of performance would be the same.

With the presentation of this model, we conclude the review of our own research on the nature of acting expertise. However, professional actors have also been utilized occasionally in the investigation of other issues, such as the universality of emotions and the influence of vicarious experience on the immune system. These studies, plus some recent experiments on acting expertise by other investigators, are reviewed briefly in chapter 12.

12

Other Investigations of Actors and Acting

Ekman and his associates (e.g., Ekman, 1992; Ekman, Hager, & Friesen, 1981; Ekman et al., 1983; Levenson, Ekman, & Friesen, 1990) have studied the universality of emotion and, in some cases, used professional actors in their experiments. In one study, Ekman et al. (1983) found specificity of autonomic nervous system (ANS) arousal when actors assumed facial expressions associated with various emotions. During another study, Ekman noted:

> When asked to pose an emotion, a person can either deliberately move particular muscles, or like a Stanislavski actor, attempt to relive or imagine a situation to create the emotional experience from which the expression will flow (Ekman et al., 1981, p. 102).

However, not all professional actors today would consider themselves "Stanislavski actors," but virtually all of them would verify that they experience some genuine, situation-specific emotion on stage.

Susana Bloch, a neuroscientist, has investigated techniques for producing these emotions in actors on demand (Bloch, 1989; Bloch, Lemeignan, & Aguilera-Torres, 1991; Bloch, Orthous, & Santibanez, 1987). In one study, Bloch and her associates showed that, by duplicating the breathing patterns that accompany six emotions, actors can experience those emotions. She presented evidence for the efficacy of her procedure based on three different measures: physiological arousal, self-appraisal, and verification by independent observers (Lemeignan, Aguilera-Torres, & Bloch, 1992). Also, some European researchers have been using both heart-rate monitors and questionnaires to investigate the nature of actors' on-stage emotions (e.g., Kochnev, 1986, 1990; Konijn, 1991; Weisweiler, 1983).

In addition to these studies, a major field of current interest involves the investigation of spectators' emotional responses during the viewing of actors' performances. Typically, this research investigates empathy and identification with dramatic or fictional characters. (For a detailed discussion, see Tan, 1996.)

In a recent study directly pertinent to our own work, McLain-Allen and Graesser (1995) hypothesized that actors would differ from non-actors in terms of cognitive abilities. While no differences were found in inference generation, world knowledge, or spatial memory, actors did demonstrate superior short-term memory abilities and verbal competence as well as longer working-memory spans.

In recent years, many researchers have investigated expertise by modeling the mental processes of experts in various domains (e.g., Clancey, 1988; Hoffman, Shadbolt, Burton, & Klein, 1995; Larkin & Simon, 1987; Soloway et al., 1988; van Lehn, Jones, & Chi, 1992; Voss et al., 1983). However, some researchers have expressed doubt about whether true modeling of human cognitive processes is feasible. Dreyfus and Dreyfus (1986) argued that:

> Rule-following, symbol-manipulating machine intelligence will probably never replace human intelligence simply because we ourselves are not "thinking machines." Human beings have an intuitive intelligence that "reasoning" machines simply cannot match (p. 86).

Furthermore, Dreyfus and Dreyfus believed that the reasoning of human beings is not rule-based, particularly not the reasoning of experts. That is, although in the early stages of expertise, learners may memorize specific rules, they will increasingly rely on know-how acquired over many years of succeeding or failing in similar situations. Therefore, the progression from novice to expert takes individuals through a number of stages but only during the first stage (the novice stage) do they depend on rules. As they gain more know-how, they learn that there are times when rules must be ignored or broken.

These authors felt that yet another problem with simulating human expertise by using AI methodology is the impossibility of representing true human feelings or moods. Yet these feelings and moods are central to theatrical performance, and as Dreyfus (1981) concluded, "There is no reason to suppose that moods...can be captured in any formal web of belief" (p. 98).

However, some researchers are now attempting to create virtual reality projects in which the spectator enters an interactive world and experiences the feeling of participating in an ongoing drama. The attempt here is not so much to mimic human processes as to encourage participants to engage in the willing suspension of disbelief necessary for the illusion of reality.

THE OZ PROJECT

We have already referred to one such program of research, *The Oz Project*, at Carnegie Mellon University (e.g., Bates, 1992, 1994; Bates, Loyall, &

Reilly, 1992; Kelso et al., 1993). This project may have some interesting implications for an understanding of actors' cognitive/emotive processes because a strand of the research involves live actors and a director, interacting with a participant. The purpose of this part of the investigation is to understand how the actions of the actors affect the participant (called the "interactor"). To do this, the actors wear head-sets and receive directions on coping with the interactor's spontaneous decisions. The director, sitting at a distance from the action, issues these directions while the project investigators look on. Among other things, the researchers are trying to determine what makes the actions of the actors believable to the interacter, and how the reactions of the interactor affect the actors. The researchers believe that this information should aid them in programming a virtual world in which the user will be immersed in a preplanned narrative while at the same time being able to affect the path of that narrative by his or her own actions.

To this end, Bates and his colleagues have also developed architecture for action that is both goal directed and behavior based and have coupled this architecture with a component for "generating, representing and expressing emotion" (Bates, 1994, p. 4). The latter aspect was based on the work of Ortony, Clore, and Collins (1988), who believed that appraisal is central to emotion and tried to trace the specific cognitive processes responsible for the elicitation of different emotions. By adding this appraisal component, Bates et al. were able to create animated creatures called *Woggles* who would display an analog of an emotion in response to actions of other Woggles. For example, an analog of anger would be created if a Woggle experienced goal failure that could be attributed to another Woggle.

Ultimately, Bates is working toward combining these various strands of research into the creation of a virtual reality world in which a participant interacts with believable, emotional agents and hence partakes in a fictional, but apparently real, experience. Because one of the intermediate steps in such a project is modeling the acting process, the entire undertaking appears to merit continued attention. (For a discussion of the Oz project, see Ryan, 1996.)

FUTURE WORK

Many additional areas of research with actors seem to warrant investigation. For example, while there have been a great number of laboratory studies testing immediate recall or recall after short retention periods, there have been far fewer studies on long-term recall, and virtually none on long-term recall for lengthy, complex material. Bahrick (1984) studied retention of Spanish vocabulary and grammar from 3 months to 50 years and found rapid forgetting for the first 6 years, followed by relatively permanent storage for the next 30 years (in what he called the *permastore*) before further decline. Furthermore, he found that in order to endure for this length of time, not only did the material have to be well learned, but the learning period itself had to be lengthy. That is, a single Spanish course was of little long term benefit even to an "A" student, whereas three or four Spanish courses spread over a couple of years allowed a good student (in the absence of subsequent rehearsal) to retain much of the vocabulary and grammar over very long periods of time.

However, the learning period for a theatrical role is usually much shorter than Bahrick's (1984) study indicated was necessary for long-term storage. Furthermore, actors retain lengthy, complex material, whereas these studies (and many other of Bahrick's ground-breaking experiments) involved discrete items such as words, names, and faces (e. g., Bahrick, Bahrick, Bahrick, & Bahrick, 1993; Bahrick, Bahrick, & Wittlinger, 1975). We plan to investigate long term verbatim retention of complex material produced by the type of elaborative learning strategies used by actors.

Another area we are currently pursuing is the effect of performed actions on verbal recall. Actors learn and perform not only the exact words of the script but also the accompanying movements as developed during rehearsal. It therefore seems probable that the encoding of motoric as well as verbal cues plays a role in retrieval. Indeed, as pointed out in chapter 2, anecdotal evidence exists that actors integrate verbal and physical actions, suggesting a motoric component to their recall (Noice, 1992).

In addition to these anecdotal reports, there is a growing body of experimental evidence showing that phrases such as "mix the cards" or "open the book" are remembered better when they are actually performed than when they are acquired under standard verbal learning instructions (for reviews see Cohen, 1989; Engelkamp, 1991; Engelkamp & Zimmer, 1985; see also Engelkamp, Zimmer, Mohr, & Sellen, 1994). Because the bulk of the enactment research concerns memory for individual words or short phrases, another aspect of our proposed study would be to investigate the specific contribution that movement makes in the retrieval of lengthy, complex material.

Furthermore, the actions in almost all enactment experiments are not only extremely simple but are physical replications of the to-be-remembered phrases. Such a direct connection virtually never exists in theatrical performances. While the movement in a well-directed play frequently amplifies the meaning, it rarely duplicates it. For example, if a man walks over to the fireplace and warms his hands while asking his wife what she did that day, obviously no literal connection exists between the words and the movement. That is, the man is not "enacting" the question about his wife's doings. A pilot study carried out prior to designing this experiment indicated that highly experienced actors justify all onstage movements, whether these movements originated with the actors themselves or were suggested by the director. That is, movements always have a purpose, however subtle. Walking away from someone might indicate a desire to appear unconcerned with the matter at hand, a need for distance preparatory to making a revelation, a sudden desire for a drink from the bar or any of dozens other possible motivations. The movement is not random and is, at some level, related to the overall content of the scene; however it is virtually never a literal enactment of the accompanying words. The question is, "Will movements that are learned with verbal material but are not a direct enactment of that material also facilitate its recall?"

We are fairly confident that the answer will be in the affirmative because, in preparation for this experiment, we tested a number of actors on an informal basis by giving them cues from plays they had not performed for some months. We found that, in those cases where actors could not recall material when sitting, they could frequently retrieve the missing lines when told to move about as they did during performance. Therefore, we believe that this finding will hold true in the controlled movement experiments we are currently designing.

CONCLUSION

Throughout this book, we suggested how actors (almost always unknowingly) depend on principles that have been empirically shown to benefit retention. These include plan recognition, use of prior knowledge, reduction of arbitrariness, distinctiveness, self generation, self referencing, causality, state dependent learning, mood congruency, context effects, overlearning, and practice effects.

Furthermore, the retention of material by use of these principles is consistent with our view that training and experience may have altered the cognitive processes of actors so that role retrieval is not just an automatic process but an example of executive speech production (see Introduction for a discussion). In conclusion, we believe that acting continues to be a potent source for investigation in cognition, emotion, AI, and many other domains. Our own program has only scratched the surface of the potential for inquiry that acting offers the researcher, and we plan to continue the quest.

APPENDIX A:
SCENE FROM *THE SECOND MAN* BY S. N. BEHRMAN[*]

Background: In this scene from Act II, Scene 2, Mrs. Kendall Frayne is in the apartment of Clark Storey, the writer who is her lover and whom she is supporting. The front doorbell rings.

(Kendall goes out into the hallway and returns in a moment followed by Austin Lowe. He is in evening dress. His manner with Kendall at first is embarrassed and hesitant. Gradually, however, she puts him at ease; she has that sort of manner.)

KENDALL

Storey's dressing. I'm the first one here.

AUSTIN

Monica's not come yet?

KENDALL

No. Cigarette?

AUSTIN

Er—thanks. *(She lights it for him.)* Thanks.

KENDALL

You and I are the only prompt ones.

AUSTIN

Yes....

KENDALL

Do you know what time it is?

AUSTIN

(Looking) Ten minutes past eleven.

---

[*]From *Three Plays* by S. N. Behrman. Copyright © 1925, 1929 and renewed 1952, 1954 by S. N. Behrman. Reprinted by permission of Random House, Inc.

KENDALL

I was here promptly at eleven. Storey hadn't even begun to dress.

AUSTIN

He hadn't!

KENDALL

I'm awfully glad you came. It was lonesome. (*She smiles at him*)

AUSTIN

I—I'm glad I found *you*.

KENDALL

Why do I never see you?

AUSTIN

Er—see me?

KENDALL

Storey talks about you all the time. You're one of the few people he respects. I always ask him to bring you to my house but you never come.

AUSTIN

I'm in the laboratory such a lot.

KENDALL

I know. Still I do wish you'd come some time—and bring Miss Grey....
(*She notices him staring at* MONICA's *colored scarf which is lying across a chair.*) What is it?

AUSTIN

That scarf.

KENDALL

You know it?

AUSTIN

It's—it's Monica's.

KENDALL

You dined here with her—didn't you?

Appendix A

AUSTIN

Yes, I did.

KENDALL

Well, then—

AUSTIN

She wore it when I left with her.

KENDALL

Didn't you take her home?

AUSTIN

She told me to go home alone—to save time.

KENDALL

Well, she probably ran back to tell Storey something.

AUSTIN

(*Bitterly*) She probably did. It must have taken a long time because—when you came— Storey hadn't even begun to dress.

KENDALL

(*After a moment*) I think you can trust Storey.

AUSTIN

Can I?

KENDALL

He told me over the phone—you and Miss Grey are engaged.

AUSTIN

There's something funny about it.

KENDALL

There's something funny about most things.

AUSTIN

(*Warming to her*) Mrs. Frayne....

KENDALL

Call me Kendall.

AUSTIN

Thank you. I wonder—I wonder if Storey tells me everything. I mean—about Monica and himself.

KENDALL

Perhaps he doesn't know everything.

AUSTIN

You mean—perhaps he's in love with her and doesn't know it?

KENDALL

Doesn't know it or won't admit it—even to himself. Perhaps. (*There is a pause*)

AUSTIN

(*Abruptly*) Are you going to marry Storey?

KENDALL

I don't know.

AUSTIN

(*Naively*) I wish you would.

KENDALL

It would solve your problem, wouldn't it. It might complicate mine.

AUSTIN

I'm not even sure it would solve mine. I wish I hadn't got into this.

KENDALL

(*She stops playing*) It's comforting to know that even a scientific genius is not immune. It rather justifies a weak woman—like me.

AUSTIN

It's rotten to be this way. Wondering about everything, suspecting everybody. Why should I care if Monica came back here or not? And yet—I do.

KENDALL

(*Slowly*) I care too, Austin. Isn't it—stupid?

AUSTIN

Do you think Monica's in love with Storey?

KENDALL

You want me to tell you she isn't, don't you?

AUSTIN

Sometimes she tells me she loathes him. ...

KENDALL

That's bad.

AUSTIN

Do you think so?

KENDALL

Wouldn't it be nice if people were like molecules or electrons or whatever you work with? It would be nice for you because you understand all about those things.

AUSTIN

Molecules are mysterious but they're more predictable than Monica. They obey some sort of law.

KENDALL

(*Amused and touched by his sincerity*) I think you're charming, Austin.

Appendix B: Protocol of T. D.

Protocol Statement #	Utterance
1	To learn the scene *The Second Man*, I think I begin first— [after reading it through the first time]—to go back the beginning and go to where the first unit or beat ends.
2	Skimming it I think that is probably at "He hadn't!". That's where the emotion seems to change.
3	Looking back, to prepare the scene—there is a clue in Austin's second line: "Thanks. Er—thanks." The "er" suggests some kind of hesitancy and suggests his mind is preoccupied. I'd have to use that as a clue.
4	Let's see...
5	And using that as a clue, the first line: "Monica's not come yet?" becomes a more emotionally charged question. There's a reason he needs to know that now.
6	The time seems to be important—but not as important.
7	So, the scene starts with an emotionally charged question, and then it kind of lulls. It starts at a high point and goes downward in intensity, and then comes sharply back up at "He hadn't."
8	And then knowing those things then I begin to learn the lines, comfortably, in sort of a semimemorization.
9	And the final thing to do then would be—that I would do—would be to put some mental pictures in my mind of the people's positions on the stage.
10	It says, "they both sit". I see him not sitting with *her*, however. Or maybe sitting down afterwards, feeling he needs to.
11	I can see him standing back up when he says, "He hadn't." I'd use all those cues, I think.
12	Moving on to the second beat, start with, as I said, right after "he hadn't," and I think it ends very soon, right after "Thank you," possibly after, "Er see me," but probably after "thank you."
13	The first line, "I, I'm glad I found you," he's obviously still irate (or not irate), still very tense, preoccupied.
14	"She smiles at him." In the scene that parenthetical comment at the end of Kendall's line is an important clue because that tells me *why* he says, "I, I'm glad I found you," why he stammers. Something about her smile, the way she smiles at him, sets him off-guard.
15	It might possibly be in connection with the words, "It was lonesome," suggesting some sort of romantically charged statement that we don't know exactly what it is yet. So I take that emotional cue.

16	I probably,—In my mind I see a physical movement there as well: The actor *might* move away a little bit. She seems to be coming on a touch strong.
17	Let's see.
18	The longer line, Kendall's longer line, has a clue in it about what this scene is about, and what this guy's trying to do.
19	Because it is longer, there must be something important in it.
20	She says he never comes to the house. That must be important because obviously these people all know each other.
21	So he has to find an excuse.
22	Obviously, by this time we see that Austin is hiding something. He's got some kind of hidden agenda going on.
23	I can see him trying to *divert* the conversation.
24	That and the movement of this one seems to start out slowly and peak in the middle on "see me" and then come back down by the time we get to "thank you."
25	There are often keys into the other people's lines.
26	The hyphenation between "time" and "and" in Kendall's line," —and bring Ms. Grey" suggests that "—and bring Ms. Grey" is a different, carries a different intention with it than time, than what comes before it.
27	"And bring Ms. Grey" is what sets off causes. It's the action that causes the *reaction* in Austin's line "thank you" with what we have later in the scene.
28	The "thank you" then takes on a different meaning, a different emotional charge, possibly cynical.
29	So putting those emotional contents to it plus the visualization of possible movement are the cues for how the lines are.
30	By this time I'm also noticing, he seems to stammer a lot. That's a clue to the rhythm of his speech which is extremely important. His rhythm is going to set the internal rhythm
31	And once I establish and adapt that internal rhythm, it will help me with memorization immensely.
32	It will also help me direct how I'm going to transform my body physically: how Austin walks, how he moves, whether he's smooth or slow, or jerky or fast in his movements. I suspect that he's possibly slightly not, I don't think he's fluid in his movements.
33	By the same, [he] has his nonfluid speech.
34	Next section.
35	Starting with him noticing Monica's colored scarf and going on, scanning here, to the end of his line "Storey hadn't even begun to dress."
36	The first thing I noticed about this is he only stammers once in this section which probably means it's a higher emotional intensity level. The words are more important.

Appendix B

37	There are a lot of monosyllabic words in here suggesting a very pointed, emotional, forceful delivery. The first one, "That scarf." Also a lot of plosive consonants. I see a lot of t's. I see some fricatives: with the f's, d's. All those things tell me there is an emotional charge and a point to the words, and that gives me a clue to the emotional intensity
38	and that gives me a clue to learning. Gives me more cues to draw on in trying to learn this.
39	"It's—it's Monica's". That's the crux of the whole scene. That's the high point of the scene, I think. Some people might put it at "that scarf," but I think it's on, "It's—it's Monica's."
40	I think the delivery here is very quick. "What is it?" "That scarf." "You know it?" "It's—" *(that one's slow)* "it's—Monica's." "You dined here with her?" "Yes
41	I'm not sure how much he shows that on the outside, but that's what's going on inside.
42	And that's what's important in learning a scene, preparing a scene.
43	There's obviously a real, he never really. ah…The punctuation gives us a clue here. We never get an exclamation point. We never get capitalization. So that probably tells me that he's trying to remain in control, which is even more important, he's trying to remain in control but actually, he's very out of control,
44	which is a dynamically charged dramatic situation that you always look for, when the opposite is appearing on the outside to what's going on in the inside.
45	It probably leaves, well…
46	"Bitterly" is another clue (a parenthetical comment) because that's the same bitterness is …, the outside being calm but betraying the anger on the inside.
47	Again there are some wonderful onomatopoeic things in that last speech after bitterly. "She probably *did*." "It must have taken a long time because when you came, Storey hadn't even begun to dress." Nice sound: the s sound, the snake sound is an onomatopoeic, a wonderful device there.
48	I'd pick that out immediately when I learn it.
49	Again, now we go on to the next section.
50	I think going from "Can I" or "I think you can trust Storey" to—*there is a pause* after Kendall's line.
51	Now we've switched. He's trying to elicit information, he's trying to get something from her. He's given out the fact, what he's after. Earlier, he said, he wants to know what's going on with Monica and Storey, and now we've switched. He's in an inquisitive mode. He's trying to—(if you want to talk about intentions), he's trying to get her to divulge what she thinks. He's trying to investigate, or some such thing. So the question is, "Can I?"
52	"There's something funny about it", is basically an open-ended statement. There's no specifics in it. So it can be interpreted in a number of ways, and it's a leading statement.

53	Obviously now, in this section again, there is another leading statement, implied question after "thank you." "I wonder—I wonder if Storey tells me everything. " —Implied question. — "I mean—about Monica and himself." Another implied question.
54	His focus now, and his intention—or his ... he's no longer preoccupied with Monica: Now he's focused on Kendall.
55	He wants to know what she knows and what she thinks.
56	And that's very important.
57	Because now I can see in my mind him almost stalking her. It seems to have a circular movement where she still might be sitting down, and he seems to come at her from different directions,
58	almost interrogating. Maybe that's a better intention for this beat: is to interrogate.
59	I noticed the words are longer. We have polysyllabic words. They tend to have a more singing quality to them, which gives it something, almost soothing; he's almost trying to sooth her to get her to feel at ease to answer his questions.
60	We have that clue earlier in the parenthetical comment that says,,"warming to her" before Mrs. Frayne. Is it possible that "warming to her" is an act? Is he warming to her in order to find out what she knows? That's my guess.
61	And that's the emotional content or context, I guess I should say
62	And then he asks the question which he already knows the answer to but he's putting it to her, "You mean, perhaps he's in love with her and doesn't know it?" That's what he thinks but he asks her the question anyway, as if she's going to confirm it.
63	But she doesn't give him any stable answer. "Perhaps." So his tactic of trying to find out the truth from her isn't working. So now he's got to change. He's got to change intention after that pause.
64	So the next beat starts there.
65	I think it ends after "and yet I do."
66	I think this beat is about honesty. I think he's divulging, maybe it's *to divulge*, I don't know, *to reveal*. It's a way of giving her a little bit of what he thinks, to see what she thinks in return.
67	It didn't work before, to lead her on into questions, so now if I give her a few bits, will she open up to me?
68	He asks her abruptly, "Are you going to marry Storey?" It's another emotional charge there.
69	So we start out with a high point in this beat, and it's probably fast. "I wish you would." "I'm not even sure it would solve mine." "I wish I hadn't got into this."
70	He is, I don't know if its subconscious, or he is sub-something; he's hiding the fact that he's trying to get something from her. He's leading her in a subtle way.
71	Before he was talking about, - a lot *toward* her, and now he's talking about *I*'s. "I wish," "I am not sure," "I, I, I." "Why do I care? Yet, I do."

Appendix B

72	There's a…, the…, his longer line starting with "It's rotten to be this way," is very important because we've got so many clauses in here.
73	We need to differentiate between each clause in some way so that they aren't the same and have the same content. Because you can't memorize them with all the same content; otherwise it's just rote learning.
74	And the more clues you have to each one, the more context you have; the faster you memorize it and the more natural it comes out.
75	"It's rotten to be this way" is a rather direct statement revealing his emotion,
76	extrapolates on it but in a more desperate emotional content, "wondering about everything, suspecting everybody."
77	Then we get back to cynicism or possibly a bitterness
78	"And yet" — dash, probably a long pause because that whole line builds.
79	It starts, "It's rotten to be this way, wondering about everything, suspecting everybody. Why should I care if Monica came back here or not, and yet, —" or maybe, "and yet" — full pause —"I do."
80	And by taking that down low, we've set it off from everything else that's come before and given it an extra emotional punch.
81	And that's something I will remember immediately. That's no problem to memorize because it has such an emotional content to it.
82	Let's see.
83	And I think the last beat here, the last thing happens.
84	It's them beginning to see each other, and beginning to joke—ah, it's a little sense of humor, a kind of a shared misery. "Do you think Monica's in love with Storey?" is probably, ah … wry —
85	And this next line is probably the same thing.
86	They're longer lines. Not too many plosives.
87	And it's a very open, kind of vulnerable feeling to it. I can see them getting closer in my mind as they talk,
88	whereas on "I do," I think he's probably had to turn away from her in that line,
89	or he's really removed himself from her and now there is a physical movement toward getting closer together.
90	In terms of an intention to put to it: *to comfort*,
91	Then we get the affirmation of that in the last line, "I think you're charming, Austin."
92	Those would be the first things I would do in memorizing or learning,
93	beginning to take apart the scene, to learn it as a prelude to memorizing it, and performing it or auditioning it.
94	The more clues, cues, memory cues I can provide myself, the more of a complete holistic environment I can sensorially, in a sensory way,

(cont.)

94 (cont.)	give myself, whether its the sound of his voice with the tempo, or it's the visualization of body positions, or whether it's the emotional cue, a kinesthetic response to various emotions, and the muscle tension of…giving it various emotional cues, the more I can flesh out his whole world.
95	The more it becomes clear to me, the easier it is to learn, the more natural it will seem.
96	So I hope this will give you some useful information.

Appendix C: Sample Page of an Annotated Script

MALE ROLE: JOE   GOAL

JOE:	(Joe turns to Mary) Is the name Mabel Lepescu?	
MARY:	What name?	
JOE:	The name the initials ML stand for. The initials on your bag.	
MARY:	No.	
JOE:	(After a long pause) Margie Longworthy? Midge Laurie?	To strike up a conversation
MARY:	(Shaking her head) No. You're not even close.	
JOE:	My initials are J. T.	
MARY:	(Pause) John?	
JOE:	No.	
MARY:	Joseph, maybe?	
JOE:	Well, not exactly. That's my first name but everybody calls me Joe. The last name is the tough one; I'll help you a little. I'm Irish. (Pause) Is it just plain Mary?	To take advantage of her joining the game
MARY:	Yes it is. I'm Irish too. At least on my father's side. English on my mother's side.	

References

Abbott, V., & Black, J. B. (1986). Goal-related inferences in comprehension. In J. A. Galambos, R. P. Abelson, & J. B. Black (Eds.), *Knowledge structures*, pp. 123–142. Hillsdale, NJ: Lawrence Erlbaum Associates.
Abbott, V., Black, J. B., & Smith, E. E. (1985). The representation of scripts in memory. *Journal of Memory and Language, 24*, 179–199.
Albrecht, J. E., O'Brien, E. J., Mason, R. A., & Myers, J. L. (1995). The role of perspective in the accessibility of goals during reading. *Journal of Experimental Psychology: Human Learning and Memory, 21*, 364–372.
Albright, H. D. (1947). *Working up a part*. Boston: Houghton Mifflin.
Aldridge, J. S. (1993). The tradition of American actor training and its current practice in undergraduate education. (Doctoral dissertation, University of Colorado at Boulder, 1993). *Dissertation Abstracts International, 54*, 735.
Anderson, J. R., & Reder, L. M. (1979). An elaborate processing explanation of depth of processing. In L. S. Cermak & F. I. M Craik (Eds.), *Levels of processing in human memory*, (pp. 385–403). Hillsdale, NJ: Lawrence Erlbaum Associates.
Anderson, R. C., & Pichert. J. W. (1978). Recall of previously unrecallable information following a shift in perspective. *Journal of Verbal Learning and Verbal Behavior, 17*, 1–12.
Anzai, Y., & Simon, H. A. (1979). The theory of learning by doing. *Psychological Review, 36*, 124–140.
Asch, S. E., & Ebenholz, S. M. (1962). The process of free recall: Evidence for non-associate factors in acquisition and retention. *Journal of Psychology, 54*, 3–31.
Bahrick, H. P. (1984). Semantic memory content in permastore: Fifty years of memory for Spanish learned in school. *Journal of Experimental Psychology: General, 113*(1), 1–29.
Bahrick, H. P., Bahrick, L. E., Bahrick, A. S., & Bahrick, P. O. (1993). Maintenance of foreign language vocabulary and the spacing effect. *Psychological Science, 4*(5), 316–321.
Bahrick, H. P., Bahrick, P. O., & Wittlinger, R. P. (1975). Fifty years of memory for names and faces: A cross-sectional approach. *Journal of Experimental Psychology: General, 104*, 54–75.
Barsalou, L. W. (1992). *Cognitive psychology: An overview for cognitive scientists*. Hillsdale, NJ: Lawrence Erlbaum Associates.
Bates, J. (1992). Virtual reality, art, and entertainment. *Presence: Teleoperators and Virtual Environments, 1* (1), 133–138.
Bates, J. (1994, April). The role of emotion in believable agents. Pittsburgh: Carnegie Mellon University. (Tech. Report CMU-CS-94-136.)
Bates, J., Loyall, A. B., & Reilly, W. S. (1992). An architecture for action, emotion and social behavior. Pittsburgh: Carnegie Mellon University. (Tech. Report CMU-CS-94-144.)
Begg, I., Vinski, E., Frankovich, L., & Holgate, B. (1991). Generating makes words memorable, but so does effective reading. *Memory & Cognition, 19*(5), 487–497.
Behrman, S. N. (1952). *Four plays by S. N. Behrman*. New York: Random House.
Bellezza, F. S. (1981). Mnemonic devices: Classification, characteristics and criteria. *Review of Educational Research, 51*, 247–275.
Bellezza, F. S., Richards, D. L., & Geiselman, R. E. (1976). Semantic processing and organization in free recall. *Memory & Cognition, 4*, 415–421.
Benedetti, R. L. (1994). *The actor at work* (6th ed.). Englewood Cliffs, NJ: Prentice Hall.
Black, J. B., & Bower, G. H. (1980). Story understanding as problem-solving. *Poetics, 9*, 223–250.
Black, J. B., Turner, T. J., & Bower, G. H. (1979). Point of view in narrative comprehension, memory, and production. *Journal of Verbal Learning and Verbal Behavior, 18*, 187–198.
Bloch, S. (1989). Effector patterns of basic human emotions: an experimental model for emotional induction. *Behavioural Brain Research, 33*, 317.
Bloch, S., Lemeignan, M., & Aguilera-Torres, N. (1991). Specific respiratory patterns distinguish among human basic emotions. *International Journal of Psychophysiology, 11*, 141–154.
Bloch, S., Orthous, P., & Santibañez-H, G. (1987). Effector patterns of basic emotions: A psychophysiological method for training actors. *Journal of Social & Biological Structures, 10*, 1–19.
Bower, G. H. (1970). Analysis of a mnemonic device. *American Scientist, 58*, 496–510.

Bower, G. H. (1982). Plans and goals in understanding episodes. In A. Flammer & W. Kintsch (Eds.), *Discourse Processing*. New York: North-Holland.
Bower, G. H. (1989). Mental models in text understanding. In A. F. Bennet & K. M. McConkey (Eds.), *Cognition in individual and social contexts* (pp. 129–144). Amsterdam, The Netherlands: Elsevier.
Bower, G. H., & Clark, M. C. (1969). Narrative stories as mediators for serial learning. *Psychonomic Science, 14*, 181–182.
Bower, G. H., Clark, M., Winzenz, D., & Lesgold, A. (1969). Hierarchical retrieval schemes in recall of categorized word lists. *Journal of Verbal Learning and Verbal Behavior, 8*, 232–343.
Bower, G. H., & Morrow, D. G. (1990). Mental models in narrative comprehension. *Science, 247*, 44–48.
Bransford, J. D., & Johnson, M. K. (1972). Contextual prerequisites for understanding: Some investigations of comprehension and recall. *Journal of Verbal Learning and Verbal Behavior, 11*, 717–726.
Brown, J. S., Collins, A., & Harris, G. (1978). Artificial intelligence and learning strategies. In H. F. O'Neil (Ed.), *Learning Strategies* (pp. 107–139). New York: Academic Press.
Bruce, B., & Newman, D. (1978). Interacting plans. *Cognitive Science, 2*, 195–233.
Bruce, B. C. (1975). *Belief systems and language understanding*. (BBN Report No. 2973). Cambridge, MA: Bolt Beranek & Newman.
Bruder, M., Cohn, L. M., Olnek, M., Pollack, N., Previto, R., & Zigler, S. (1986). *A practical handbook for the actor*. New York: Vintage Books.
Carey, D. (1995). *Master class: The actor's audition manual*. London: Nick Hern Books.
Carey, S. (1985). Are children fundamentally different kinds of thinkers and learners than adults? In S. F. Chipman, J. W. Segal, & R. Glaser (Eds.), *Thinking and learning skills: Current research and open questions* (Vol. 2, pp. 485–517). Hillsdale, NJ: Lawrence Erlbaum Associates.
Chaffin, R. (1994, July). *Memorizing for performance: A case study of a concert pianist*. Paper presented at the Third Practical Aspects of Memory Conference, University of Maryland, College Park, MD.
Charness, N., Krampe, R., & Mayr, U. (1996). The role of practice and coaching in entrepreneurial skill domains. An international comparison of life-span chess skill acquisition. In K. A. Ericsson (Ed.), *The road to excellence: The acquisition of expert performance in the arts and sciences, sports and games* (pp. 51–80). Mahwah: NJ: Lawrence Erlbaum Associates.
Chase, W. G., & Ericsson, K. A. (1982). *Skill and working memory* (Tech. Report No. 7). Pittsburgh: Carnegie-Mellon University.
Chase, W. G., & Simon, H. A. (1973). Perception in chess. *Cognitive Psychology, 4*, 55–81.
Chi, M. T. H., Bassok, M., Lewis, M. W., Reimann, P., & Glaser, R. (1989). Self-explanations: How students study and use examples in learning to solve problems. *Cognitive Science, 13*, 145–182.
Chi, M. T. H., Feltovich, P. J., & Glaser, R. (1981). Categorization and representation of physics problems by experts and novices. *Cognitive Science, 5*, 121–152.
Chi, M. T. H., Glaser, R., & Farr, M. J. (Eds.). (1988). *The nature of expertise*. Hillsdale, NJ: Lawrence Erlbaum Associates.
Chi, M. T. H., Glaser, R., & Rees, E. (1982). Expertise in problem solving. In R. J. Sternberg (Ed.), *Advances in the psychology of human intelligence* (Vol. 1, pp. 7–75). Hillsdale, NJ: Lawrence Erlbaum Associates.
Chi, M. T. H., & VanLehn, K. A. (1991). The content of physics self-explanations. *Journal of the Learning Sciences, 1*, 67–105.
Chiesi, H. L., Spilich, G. J., & Voss, J. F. (1979). Acquisition of domain-related information in relation to high and low domain knowledge. *Journal of Verbal Learning and Verbal Behavior, 18*, 257–274.
Clancey, W. C. (1988). Acquiring, representing, and evaluating a competence model of diagnostic strategy. In M. T. H. Chi, R. Glaser, & M. J. Farr (Eds.), *The nature of expertise* (pp. 343–418). Hillsdale, NJ: Lawrence Erlbaum Associates.
Clark, H. H., & Clark, E. V. (1977). *Psychology and language: An introduction to psycholinguistics*. New York: Harcourt Brace.
Cofer, C. N. (1941). A comparison of logical and verbatim learning of prose passages of different lengths. *American Journal of Psychology, 54*, 1-20.
Cohen, R. (1992). *Acting one*. Mountain View, CA: Mayfield.
Cohen, R. L. (1989). Memory for action events: The power of enactment. *Educational Psychology Review, 1*, 57-80.
Craik, F. I. M., & Tulving, E. (1975). Depth of processing and the retention of words in episodic memory. *Journal of Experimental Psychology: General, 104*, 268-294.
Craik, F. I. M., & Watkins, M. J. (1973). The role of rehearsal in short-term memory. *Journal of Verbal Learning and Verbal Behavior, 12*, 599-607.

References

Dellarosa, D., & Bourne, L. E., Jr. (1984). Decisions and memory: Differential retrievability of consistent and contradictory evidence. *Journal of Verbal Learning and Verbal Behavior, 23,* 669-682.
Dolman, J., Jr. (1928). *The art of play production.* New York: Harper & Brothers.
Dreyfus, H. L. (1981). From micro-worlds to knowledge representation: AI at an impasse. In J. Haugeland (Ed.), *Mind design: Philosophy, psychology, artificial intelligence* (pp. 161–204). Cambridge, MA: MIT Press.
Dreyfus, H., & Dreyfus, S. (1986, Summer). Why expert systems do not exhibit expertise. *IEEE Expert,* 86–90.
Ebbinghaus, H. (1913). *Memory: A contribution to experimental psychology.* New York: Teachers College, Columbia University. (Original work published 1885.)
Egan, D. E., & Schwartz, B. J. (1979). Chunking in recall of symbolic drawings. *Memory & Cognition, 7,* 149–158.
Einstein, G. O., & Hunt, R. R. (1980). Levels of processing and organization: Additive effects of individual-item and relational processing. *Journal of Experimental Psychology: Human Learning and Memory, 6,* 588–598.
Ekman, P. (1992). Facial expressions of emotion: New findings, new questions. *Psychological Science, 3*(1), 34–38.
Ekman, P., Hager, J. C., & Friesen, W. V. (1981). The symmetry of emotional and deliberate facial actions. *Psychophysiology, 18,* 101–106.
Ekman, P., Levenson, R. W., & Friesen, W. V. (1983). Autonomic nervous system activity distinguishes among emotions. *Science, 221,* 1208–1210.
Engelkamp, J. (1991). Memory of action events: Some implications for memory theory and for imagery. In C. Cornoldi & M. A. McDaniel (Eds.), *Imagery and cognition.* New York: Springer-Verlag.
Engelkamp, J., & Zimmer, H. D. (1985). Motor programs and their relation to semantic memory. *German Journal of Psychology, 9,* 239–254.
Engelkamp, J., Zimmer, H. D., Mohr, G., & Sellen, O. (1994). Memory of self-performed tasks: Self-performing during recognition. *Memory & Cognition, 22*(1), 34–39.
Equity News. Annual report on employment, membership & finances. (1994, December).
Ericsson, K. A. (1988). Concurrent verbal reports on text comprehension. *Text, 8*(4), 295–325.
Ericsson, K. A., & Charness, N. (1994). Expert performance: Its structure and acquisition. *American Psychologist, 49*(8), 725–747.
Ericsson, K. A., Krampe, R. T., & Tesch-Roemer, C. (1993). The role of deliberate practice in the acquisition of expert performance. *Psychological Review, 100*(3), 363–406.
Ericsson, K. A., & Lehmann, A. C. (1996). Expert and exceptional performance: Evidence of maximal adaptation to task constraints. *Annual Review of Psychology, 47,* 273–305.
Ericsson, K. A., Lehmann, A. C., & Taylor, J. A. (1993, November). *The acquisition and structure of music sight-reading.* Poster session presented at the thirty-fourth annual meeting of the Psychonomic Society, Washington, DC.
Ericsson, K. A., & Polson, P. G. (1988). A cognitive analysis of exceptional memory for restaurant orders. In M.T.H. Chi, R. Glaser, & M.J. Farr (Eds.), *The nature of expertise* (pp. 23–70). Hillsdale, NJ: Lawrence Erlbaum Associates.
Ericsson, K. A., & Simon, H. A. (1984). *Protocol analysis: Verbal reports as data.* Cambridge, MA: MIT Press.
Ericsson, K. A., & Simon, H. A. (1993). *Protocol analysis: Verbal reports as data* (Rev. ed.). Cambridge, MA: MIT Press.
Fletcher, C. R. (1984). *Strategies for the allocation of short-term memory during comprehension.* Unpublished doctoral dissertation, University of Colorado, Denver.
Fletcher, C. R., & Bloom, C. P. (1988). Casual reasoning in the comprehension of simple narrative texts. *Journal of Memory and Language, 27,* 235–244.
Franklin, M., & Dixon, J. (1938). *Rehearsal.* Englewood Cliffs, NJ: Prentice Hall.
Frase, L. T. (1975). Prose processing. In G. H. Bower (Ed.), *The psychology of learning and motivation: Advances in research and theory.* New York: Academic Press.
Funke, L., & Booth, J. E. (1961). *Actors talk about acting.* New York: Avon Books.
Futterman, A. D., Kemeny, M. E., Shapiro, D., Polonsky, W., & Fahey, J. L. (1992). Immunological variability associated with experimentally-induced positive and negative affective states. *Psychological Medicine, 22,* 231–238.

Gentner, D., & Gentner, D. R. (1983). Flowing waters or teeming crowds: Mental models of electricity. In D. Gentner & A.L. Stevens (Eds.), *Mental models* (pp 99–129). Hillsdale, NJ: Lawrence Erlbaum Associates.
Gitomer, D. H., & Glaser, R. (1987). Knowledge, self-regulation and instruction. In R. E. Snow & M. J. Farr (Eds.). *Aptitude, learning, and instruction* (pp. 301–325). Hillsdale, N:J: Lawrence Erlbaum Associates.
Glaser, R. (1984, February). Education and thinking: The role of knowledge. *American Psychologist*, 39(2), 93-104.
Glaser, R. (1987). Thoughts on expertise. In C. Schooler & K. W. Schaie (Eds.), *Cognitive functioning and social structure over the life course* (pp. 81–94). Norwood, NJ: Ablex.
Glenberg, A. M., Meyer, M., & Lindem, K. (1987). Mental models contribute to foregrounding during text comprehension. *Journal of Memory and Language*, 26, 69–83.
Glenn, S. L. (1977). *The complete actor.* Boston, MA: Allyn & Bacon.
Goodman, E. (1956). *Make believe—The art of acting.* New York: Scribner.
Gordon, P., Valentine, E., & Wilding, J. (1984). One man's memory: A study of a mnemonist. *British Journal of Psychology*, 75, 1–14.
Graesser, A. C. (1981). *Prose comprehension beyond the word.* New York: Springer-Verlag.
Graesser, A. C., Bowers, C. A., & Bommareddy, S. B. (1995, November). Who knows what? Tracking knowledge in narrative. Paper presented at the thirty-sixth annual meeting of the Psychonomic Society, Los Angeles, CA.
Graesser, A. C., & Clark, L. F. (1985). *The structures and procedures of implicit knowledge.* Norwood, NJ: Ablex.
Graesser, A. C., Singer, M., & Trabasso, T. (1994). Constructing inferences during narrative text comprehension. *Psychological Review*, 101, 371–395.
Graves, B., & Frederiksen, C. H. (1991). Literary expertise in the description of a fictional narrative. *Poetics*, 20, 1–26.
Grice, H. P. (1975). Logic and conversation. In P. Cole and J. Morgan (Eds.), *Syntax and semantics* (Vol. 3). New York: Academic Press.
Grote, D. (1985). *Script analysis: Reading and understanding the playscript for production.* Belmont, CA: Wadsworth.
Gruneberg, M. M. (1978). The feeling of knowing, memory blocks, and memory aids. In M. M. Gruneberg & P. Morris (Eds.), *Aspects of memory.* London: Methuen.
Hagen, U. (1973). *Respect for acting.* New York: Macmillan.
Hagen, U. (1991). *A challenge for the actor.* New York: Scribner's.
Hasher, L., & Griffin, M. (1978). Reconstructive and reproductive processes in memory. *Journal of Experimental Psychology: Human Learning and Memory*, 4, 318–330.
Hecht, B., & McArthur, C. (1949). The front page. In J. Gassner, (Ed.), *Twenty-five best plays of the modern American theatre.* New York: Crown Publishers.
Hemingway, E. (1928). *Men without women.* Harmondsworth, England: Penguin Books.
Herrmann, D. (1987). Task appropriateness of mnemonic techniques. *Perceptual and Motor Skills*, 64, 171–178.
Herrmann, D. J. (1991). *Super memory.* Emmaus, PA: Rodale Press.
Higbee, K. L. (1988). *Your memory: How it works and how to improve it.* New York: Paragon House.
Hinsley, D. A., Hayes, J. R., & Simon, H. A. (1977). From words to equations: Meaning and representation in algebra word problem. In M. A. Just & P. A. Carpenter (Eds.), *Cognitive processes in comprehension* (pp. 89–108). Hillsdale, NJ: Lawrence Erlbaum Associates.
Hjelmquist, E. (1984). Memory for conversations. *Discourse Processes*, 7, 321–336.
Hjelmquist, E., & Gidlund, Å. (1985). Free recall of conversations. *Text*, 5(3), 169–185.
Hoffman, R. R., Shadbolt, N. R., Burton, A. M., & Klein, G. (1995). Eliciting knowledge from experts: A methodological analysis. *Organizational Behavior and Human Decision Processes*, 62(2), 129–158.
Hunt, R. R., & Einstein. G. O. (1981). Relational and item-specific information in memory. *Journal of Verbal Learning and Verbal Behavior*, 20, 497–514.
Intons-Peterson, M. J., & Smyth, M. M. (1987). The anatomy of repertory memory. *Journal of Experimental Psychology: Learning, Memory, and Cognition*, 13, 490–500.
Jacoby, L. L. (1978). On interpreting the effects of repetition: Solving a problem versus remembering a solution. *Journal of Verbal Learning and Verbal Behavior*, 17, 649–667.
Jacoby, L. L., Craik, F. I. M., & Begg, I. (1979). Effects of decision difficulty on recognition and recall. *Journal of Verbal Learning and Verbal Behavior*, 18, 585–600.

References

Johnson, R. E. (1970). Recall of prose as a function of the structural importance of the linguistic units. *Journal of Verbal Learning and Verbal Behavior, 9*, 12–20.
Johnson-Laird, P. N. (1983). *Mental models*. Cambridge, England: Cambridge University Press.
Kahneman, D. (1973). *Attention and effort*. Englewood Cliffs, NJ: Prentice-Hall.
Kay, D. S., & Black, J. B. (1986). Explanation-driven processing in summarization: The interaction of content and process. In J. B. Galambos, R. P. Abelson, & J. B. Black (Eds.), *Knowledge structures* (pp. 211–236). Hillsdale, NJ: Lawrence Erlbaum Associates.
Keenan, J. M., Baillet, S. D., & Brown, P. (1984). The effect of causal cohesion on comprehension and memory. *Journal of Verbal Learning and Verbal Behavior, 23*, 115–126.
Keenan, J. M., MacWhinney, B., & Mayhew, D. (1977). Pragmatics in memory: A study of natural conversation. *Journal of Verbal Learning and Verbal Behavior, 16*, 549–560.
Kelso, M. T, Weyhrauch, P., & Bates, J. (1993). Dramatic presence. *Presence, 2*(1), 1–15.
Kintsch, W. (1977). On comprehending stories. In M. A. Just & P. Carpenter (Eds.), *Cognitive processes in comprehension*. Hillsdale, NJ: Lawrence Erlbaum Associates.
Kintsch, W., & Bates, E. (1977). Recognition memory for statements from a classroom lecture. *Journal of Experimental Psychology: Human Learning and Memory, 3*, 150–159.
Kintsch, W., & van Dijk, T. A. (1975). Recalling and summarizing stories. *Language, 40*, 98–116.
Kirk, J. W. , & Bellas, R. A. (1985). *The art of directing*. Belmont, CA: Wadsworth Publishing.
Kochnev, V. I. (1986). Investigation of dynamics characteristics, emotional reactivity in connection with the issue of actors' gifts. *Problems of Psychology, 5*, 153–160.
Kochnev, V. I. (1990). The stage emotional experience: Attempt at the solution of the problem. *The Soviet Journal of Psychology, 11*(4), 56–69.
Konijn, E. A. (1991). What's on between the author and his audience? Empirical analysis of emotion processes in the theatre. In G. D. Wilson (Ed.), *Psychology and the performing arts* (pp. 59–73). Lisse, The Netherlands: Swets & Zeitlinger.
Krebs, E. W., Snowman, J, & Smith, S. H. (1978). Teaching new dogs old tricks: Facilitating prose learning through mnemonic training. *Journal of Instructional Psychology, 5*, 33–39.
Kucera, H., & Francis, W. N. (1967). *Computational analysis of present-day American English*. Providence, RI: Brown University Press.
Lachman, R. & Field, W. H. (1965). Recognition and recall of verbal material as a function of degree of training. *Psychonomic Science, 2*, 225–226.
Larkin, J. H., & Simon, H. A. (1987). Why a diagram is (sometimes) worth ten thousand words. *Cognitive Science, 11*, 65–99.
Lemeignan, M., Aguilera-Torres, N., & Bloch, S. (1992). Emotional effector patterns: Recognition of expressions. *European Bulletin of Cognitive Psychology, 12*, 173–188.
Lesgold, A. M. (1984). Acquiring expertise. In J. R. Anderson & S. M. Kosslyn (Eds.), *Tutorials in learning and memory: Essays in honor of Gordon Bower* (pp. 31–60). San Francisco: Freeman.
Lesgold, A. M., Feltovich, P. J., Glaser, R., & Wang, Y. (1981). *The acquisition of perceptual diagnostic skill in radiology* (Tech. Report PDS-1). Pittsburgh: Learning Research and Development Center, University of Pittsburgh.
Levenson, R. W., Ekman, P., & Friesen, W. V. (1990). Voluntary facial action generates emotion-specific autonomic nervous system activity. *Psychophysiology, 27*, 363–384.
Lichtenstein, E. H., & Brewer, W. F. (1989). Memory for goal-directed events. *Cognitive Psychology, 12*, 412–445.
Loisette, A. (1899). *Assimilative memory, or how to attend and never forget*. New York: Funk & Wagnalls.
Long, D. B., Seely, M. R., & Oppy, B. J. (1996). The availability of causal information during reading. *Discourse Processes, 22*, 145–170.
Lorayne, H. (1957). *How to develop a super-power memory*. New York: Frederick Fell.
Lorayne, H. (1985). *Page-a-minute memory book*. New York: Ballantine.
Lorayne, H. (1988). *Memory makes money*. Boston, MA: Little, Brown.
Lorayne, H. (1990). *Super memory—super student: How to raise your grades in 30 days*. Boston, MA: Little, Brown.
Lorayne, H. & Lucas, J. (1974). *The memory book*. New York: Ballantine.
Macauley, R., & Lanning, G. (1964). *Technique in fiction*. New York: Harper & Row.
Mandler, G. (1967). Organization and memory. In K. W. Spence & J. T. Spence (Eds.), *The psychology of learning and motivation* (Vol. 1). New York: Academic Press.
Mantyla, T. (1986). Optimizing cue effectiveness. Recall of 500 and 600 incidentally learned words. *Journal of Experimental Psychology: Learning, Memory and Cognition, 15*, 710–720.

Marsalis, W. (1996). *Masters of American music.* New York: BRAVO. (Broadcast on February 27, 1996.)
McDaniel, M. A. (1981). Syntactic complexity and elaborative processing. *Memory & Cognition, 9,* 487–495.
McDaniel, M. A., & Einstein, G. (1989). Material-appropriate processing: A contextualist approach to reading and studying strategies. *Educational Psychology Review, 1,* 113–145.
McGaw, C. (1955). *Acting is believing: A basic method.* New York: Holt, Rinehart & Winston.
McKeithen, K. B., Reitman, J. S., Reuter, H. H., & Hirtle, S. C. (1981). Knowledge organization and skill differences in computer programmers. *Cognitive Psychology, 13,* 307–325.
McKoon, G., & Ratcliff, R. (1986). Inferences about predictable events. *Journal of Experimental Psychology: Learning, Memory, and Cognition, 12,* 82–91.
McKoon, G., & Ratcliff, T. (1992). Inference during reading. *Psychological Review, 99,* 440–446.
McKoon, G., Ratcliff, R., & Dell, G.S. (1986). A critical evaluation of the semantic-episodic distinction. *Journal of Experimental Psychology: Learning, Memory, and Cognition, 12*(2), 295–306.
McLain-Allen, B., & Graesser, A. C. (1995, June). *Differences in cognitive abilities between actors and non-actors.* Poster presented at the seventh annual convention of the American Psychological Society, New York, NY.
McTeague, J. (1993). *Before Stanislavsky: American professional acting schools and acting theory, 1875-1925.* Metuchen, NJ: The Scarecrow Press.
Meisner, S., & Longwell. D. (1987). *Sanford Meisner on acting.* New York: Vintage Books.
Mekler, E. (1987). *The new generation of acting teachers.* New York: Viking Penguin.
Miller, G. A. (1973). Psychology and communication. In G. A. Miller (Ed.), *Communication, language and meaning: Psychological perspectives* (pp. 3–12). New York: Basic Books.
Milner, M., & Danielson, J. (1995, April). *The accuracy with which professional actors perform different theatrical roles.* Paper presented at National Conference on Undergraduate Research, Union College, Schenectady, NY.
Nisbett, R. E., & Wilson, T. D. (1977). Telling more than we can know: Verbal reports on mental processes. *Psychological Review, 84,* 231–259.
Noice, H. (1991). The role of explanations and plan recognition in the learning of theatrical scripts. *Cognitive Science, 15,* 425–460.
Noice, H. (1992). Elaborative memory strategies of professional actors. *Applied Cognitive Psychology, 6,* 417–427.
Noice, H. (1993). Effects of strategy on the on the verbatim retention of theatrical script. *Applied Cognitive Psychology, 7,* 75–84.
Noice, H., & Noice, T. (1993a). The effects of segmentation on the recall of theatrical material. *Poetics, 22,* 51–67.
Noice, H., & Noice, T. (1993b). Facilitation of recall through organization of theatrical material. *Proceedings of the Fifteenth Annual Conference of the Cognitive Science Society* (pp. 789–793). Hillsdale, NJ: Lawrence Erlbaum Associates.
Noice, H., & Noice, T. (1994). An example of role preparation by a professional actor: A think-aloud protocol. *Discourse Processes, 18,* 345–369.
Noice, H., & Noice, T. (1996a). Two approaches to learning a theatrical script. *Memory, 4*(1), 1–17.
Noice, H., & Noice, T. (1996b). The mental processes of professional actors as examined through self-report, experimental investigation and think-aloud protocol. In M. S. MacNealy, & R. J. Kreuz (Eds.), *Empirical approaches to literature and aesthetics* (pp. 361–377). Norwood, NJ: Ablex.
Noice, H., & Noice, T. (1996c, November). *Recognition of obscure Shakespearean words in and out of context.* Paper presented at the thirty-Sixth annual meeting of the Psychonomic Society, Los Angeles, CA.
Noice, T. (1995). The application of memory and learning principles of cognitive science to an actor's ability to perform "in the moment." (Doctoral dissertation, Wayne State University, 1995). *Dissertation Abstract International, 56–05A,* 1586.
Noice, T., & Noice, H. (1997). Effort and active experiencing as factors in verbatim recall. *Discourse Processes, 23,* 51–69.
Norman, D. A. (1976). *Memory and attention* (pp. 130–156). New York: Wiley.
O'Brien, E. J., & Albrecht, J. E. (1992). Comprehension strategies in the development of a mental model. *Journal of Experimental Psychology: Human Learning and Memory, 18,* 777–784.
O'Brien, E. J., & Myers, J. L. (1985). When comprehension difficulty improves memory for text. *Journal of Experimental Psychology: Learning, Memory, and Cognition, 11,* 12–21.

References

Oliver, W. L., & Ericsson, K. A. (1986). Repertory actors' memory for their parts. *Proceedings of the Eighth Annual Conference of the Cognitive Science Society, Amherst, MA* (pp. 399–406). Hillsdale, NJ: Lawrence Erlbaum Associates.

Ortony, A., Clore, G. L., & Collins, A. (1988). *The cognitive structure of emotions.* Cambridge, MA: Cambridge University Press.

Owens, J., Bower, G. H., & Black, J. B. (1979). The "soap opera" effect in story recall. *Memory and Cognition, 7,* 185–191.

Paivio, A. (1971). *Imagery and verbal processes.* New York: Holt, Rinehart & Winston.

Pollack, S. (Executive Producer). (1984). *Sanford Meisner: The theatre's best kept secret.* Woodbury, NY: BRAVO Network.

Pressley, M., McDaniel, M. A., Turnure, J. E., Wood, E., & Ahmad, M. (1987). Generation and precision of elaboration: Effects on intentional and incidental learning. *Journal of Experimental Psychology: Learning, Memory, and Cognition, 13,* 291–300.

Pressley, M., Symons, S., McDaniel, M. A., Snyder, B. L., & Turnure, J. E. (1988). Elaborative interrogation facilitates acquisition of confusing facts. *Journal of Educational Psychology, 80,* 268–278.

Robertson, S., & Swartz, M. (1988). Why do we ask ourselves questions? *Questioning Exchange, 2,* 47–51.

Rumelhart, D. E. (1975). Notes on a schema for stories. In D. G. Collins & A. Collins (Eds.), *Representation and understanding.* New York: Academic Press.

Rundus, D. (1977). Maintenance rehearsal and single-level processing. *Journal of Verbal Learning and Verbal Behavior, 16,* 665–681.

Ryan, M.-L. (in press). Interactive drama: Narrativity in a highly interactive environment. In O'Donnel (Ed.). *Modern fiction studies* (Vol. 43). Baltimore, MD: John Hopkins University Press.

Saroyan, W. (1939). *The time of your life.* New York: Harcourt Brace.

Scardamalia, M., & Bereiter, C. (1991). Literate expertise. In K. A. Ericsson & J. Smith (Eds.), *Toward a general theory of expertise* (pp. 172–194). Cambridge, MA: Cambridge University Press.

Schmidt, C. F. (1976). Understanding human action: Recognizing the plans and motives of other persons. In J. S. Carrol & J. W. Payne (Eds.), *Cognition and social behavior.* Hillsdale, NJ: Lawrence Erlbaum Associates.

Schmidt, C. F., Sridharan, N. S., & Goodson, J. L. (1978). The plan recognition problem: An intersection of artificial intelligence and psychology. *Artificial Intelligence, 11,* 45–83.

Schneider, W., & Shiffrin, R. M. (1977). Controlled and automatic human information processing: I. Detection, search and attention. *Psychological Review, 84,* 1–66.

Searle, J. R. (1976). A classification of illocutionary acts. *Language in Society, 5,* 1–23.

Siegal, A. C., & Segal, E. M. (1995, November). *Automatic processes during narrative comprehension: Understanding point of view.* Paper presented at the thirty-Sixth annual meeting of the Psychonomic Society, Los Angeles, CA.

Silverberg, L. (1994). *The Sanford Meisner approach: An actor's workbook.* Lyme, NH: Smith and Kraus.

Simon, N. (1991). *The collected plays of Neil Simon* (Vol. 3). New York: Random House.

Sloboda, J. (1991). Musical expertise. In K. A. Ericsson & J. Smith (Eds.), *Toward a general theory of expertise* (pp. 153–171). Cambridge, MA: Cambridge University Press.

Smiley, S. (1971). *Playwriting: The structure of action.* Englewood Cliffs, NJ: Prentice-Hall.

Snowman, J., Krebs, E. U., & Lockhart, L. (1980). Improving recall of information from prose in high-risk students through learning strategy training. *Journal of Instructional Psychology,7,* 35-40.

Soloway, E., Adelson, B., & Ehrlich, K. (1988). Knowledge and processes in the comprehension of computer programs. In M. T. H. Chi, R. Glaser, & M. J. Farr (Eds.), *The nature of expertise* (pp. 129–152). Hillsdale, NJ: Lawrence Erlbaum Associates.

Solso, R. L., & Dallop, P. (1995). Prototype formation among professional dancers. *Empirical Studies of the Arts, 13*(1), 3–16.

Stanislavski, C. (1984). *An actor prepares.* New York: Theatre Arts Books. (Original work published in 1936.)

Stanislavski, C. (1985). *Building a character.* New York: Theatre Arts Books. (Original work published in 1949.)

Stanislavski, C. (1983). *Creating a role.* New York: Theatre Arts Books. (Original work published in 1961.)

Stanislavski, K. (1924). *My life in art.* New York: Theatre Arts Books.

Stanislavski, K. (1928). *My life in art.* (Rev. ed.). Moscow: Foreign Languages Publishing House.

Starkes, J. L., & Deakin, J. M. (1985). Perception in sport: A cognitive approach to skilled performance. In W. F. Straub & J. M. Williams (Eds.), *Cognitive sport psychology*. Lansing, NY: Sport Science Associates.

Staszewski, J. J. (1988). Skilled memory and expert mental calculation. In M. T. H. Chi, R. Glaser, & M. F. Farr (Eds.), *The nature of expertise*. Hillsdale, NJ: Lawrence Erlbaum Associates.

Stein, B. S., & Bransford, J. D. (1979). Constraints on effective elaboration: Effects of precision and subject generation. *Journal of Verbal Learning and Verbal Behavior*, 18, 769–777.

Stein, B. S., Littlefield, J., Bransford, J. D., & Persampieri, M. (1984). Elaboration and knowledge acquisition. *Memory and Cognition*, 12, 522–529.

Sternberg, R. J. (1996). Costs of expertise. In K. A. Ericsson (Ed.), *The road to excellence* (pp. 347–354). Mahwah, NJ: Lawrence Erlbaum Associates.

Tan, E. S. (1996). *Emotion and the structure of narrative film: Film as an emotion machine*. Hillsdale, NJ: Lawrence Erlbaum Associates.

Trabasso, T., & Magliano, J. P. (1996). Conscious understanding during comprehension. *Discourse Processes*, 21(3), 255–287.

Trabasso, T., Secco, T., & van den Broek, P. W. (1984). Causal cohesion and story coherence. In H. Mandl, N. L. Stein, & T. Trabasso (Eds.), *Learning and comprehension of text* (pp. 83–111). Hillsdale, NJ: Lawrence Erlbaum Associates.

Trabasso, T., & van den Broek, P. W. (1985). Causal thinking and the representation of narrative events. *Journal of Memory and Language*, 24, 612–630.

Trabasso, T., van den Broek, P. W., & Liu, L. (1988). A model for generating questions that assess and promote comprehension. *Questioning Exchange*, 2, 25–38.

Trabasso, T., van den Broek, P. W., & Suh, S. (1989). Logical necessity and transitivity of causal relations in the representation of stories. *Discourse Processes*, 12, 1–25.

Tulving, E. (1983). *Elements of episodic memory*. New York: Oxford University Press.

Tulving, E. (1984). Precis of elements of episodic memory. *The Behavioral and Brain Sciences*, 7, 223–268.

Tulving, E. (1985). How many memory systems are there. *American Psychologist*, 40, 385–398.

Tulving, E., & Thomson, D. M. (1973). Encoding specificity and retrieval processes in episodic memory. *Psychological Review*, 80(5), 352–373.

Tulving, E., & Watkins. O. C. (1977). Recognition failure of words with a single meaning. *Memory and Cognition*, 5, 513–522.

Tulving, E., & Wiseman, S. (1975). Relation between recognition and recognition failure of recallable words. *Bulletin of the Psychonomic Society*, 6, 79–82.

Tyler, S. W., Hertel, P. T., McCallum, M. C., & Ellis, H. C. (1979). Cognitive effort and memory. *Journal of Experimental Psychology: Human Learning and Memory*, 5, 607–617.

van den Broek, P. W. (1988). The effect of causal relations and hierarchical position on the importance of story statements. *Journal of Memory and Language*, 27, 1–22.

van den Broek, P. (1990). Causal inferences and the comprehension of narrative texts. In A. C. Graesser & G. H. Bower (Eds.), *Inferences and text comprehension*. New York: Academic Press.

van den Broek, P. W., & Trabasso, T. (1986). Causal networks versus goal hierarchies in summarizing text. *Discourse Processes*, 9, 1–15.

van Lehn, K., Jones, R. M., & Chi, M. T. (1992). A model of self-explanation effect. *The Journal of the Learning Sciences*, 2, 1–59.

Voss, J. F., Greene, T. R., Post, T. A., & Penner, B. C. (1983). Problem-solving skill in the social sciences. In G.H. Bower (Ed.), *The psychology of learning and motivation: Advances in research theory* (Vol. 17, pp. 165–213). New York: Academic Press.

Voss, J. F., & Post, T. A. (1988). On the solving of ill-structured problems. In M. T. H. Chi, R. Glaser, & M. J. Farr (Eds.), *The nature of expertise* (pp. 261–285). Hillsdale, NJ: Lawrence Erlbaum Associates.

Watkins, M. J., & Tulving, E. (1975). Episodic memory: Where recognition fails. *Journal of Experimental Psychology: General*, 104, 5–29

Weisweiler, H. (1983). *Die Belastung des Schauspielers an seinem Arbeitsplatz*. [The pressures of live theater performance on the actor.] Unpublished doctoral dissertation. Muenchener Universitaet, Theaterwissenschaft, Munich.

Wilding, J., & Valentine, E. (1985). One man's memory for prose, faces and names. *British Journal of Psychology*, 76, 215–219.

Wilding, J., & Valentine, E. (1994). Memory champions. *British Journal of Psychology*, 85, 231–244.

Woloshyn, V. E., Willoughby, T., Wood, E., & Pressley, M. (1990). Elaborative interrogation facilitates adult learning of factual paragraphs. *Journal of Educational Psychology*, 82, 513–524.

References

Zechmeister, E. B., & Nyberg, S. E. (1982). *Human memory: An introduction to research and theory.* Monterey, CA: Brooks/Cole.

Zwaan, R. A., Langston, M. D., & Graesser, A. C. (1995). The construction of situation models in narrative comprehension: An event-indexing model. *Psychological Science, 6*(5), 292–297.

Author Index

A

Abbott, V., 48, 53
Adelson, B., ix, 119
Aguilera-Torres, N., 118
Ahmad, M., 67
Albrecht, J. E., 21, 34
Albright, H. D., 2, 3
Aldridge, J. S., 5
Anderson, R. C., 21, 34, 44, 69
Anzai, Y., 56
Asch, S. E., 95

B

Bahrick, A. S., 121
Bahrick, H. P., 120, 121
Bahrick, L. E., 121
Bahrick, P. E., 121
Baillet, S. D., 96
Barsalou, L. W., xvii
Bassok, M., 33, 68
Bates, E., 19
Bates, J., x, 119, 120
Begg, I., 44, 104
Behrman, S. N., 22, 55, 71, 88
Bellas, R. A., 63
Bellezza, F. S., 78, 95
Benedetti, R. L., 6, 7
Bereiter, C., ix
Black, J. B., 21, 34, 36, 48, 53, 96
Bloch, S., 118

Bloom, C. P., 84
Bommareddy, S. B., 35
Booth, J. E., xvi
Bourne, L. E., Jr., 34
Bower, G. H., 21, 34, 48, 78, 84, 96, 110
Bowers, C. A., 35
Bransford, J. D., 17, 34, 67
Brewer, W. F., 48
Brown, J. S., x, 69
Brown, P., 96
Bruce, B., 68
Bruder, M., xiii, xvi, 4, 5
Burton, A. M., 119

C

Carey, D., x, 87
Chaffin, R., xv
Charness, N., xi, xiv
Chase, W. G., ix, 20
Chi, M. T. H., ix, x, 33, 48, 68, 119
Chiesi, H. L., 34, 48
Clancey, W. C., 119
Clark, E. V., xvii
Clark, H. H., xviii
Clark, L. F., 84
Clark, M. C., 84, 96
Clore, G. L., 120
Cofer, C. N., 23
Cohen, R., xv, 7
Cohen, R. L., 121
Cohn, L. M., xiii, xvi, 4, 5

147

Collins, A., x, 69, 120
Craik, F. I. M., 17, 44, 45

D

Dallop, P., ix, xv
Danielson, J., 111
Deakin, J. M., ix
Dell, G. S., 105
Dellarosa, D., 34
Dixon, J., 2
Dolman, J., Jr., 1, 2
Dreyfus, H. L., x, 119
Dreyfus, S., x, 119

E

Ebbinghaus, H., 2, 4, 19
Ebenholz, S. M., 95
Egan, D. E., ix
Ehrlich, K., ix, 119
Einstein, G. O., 46, 104
Ekman, P., xiv, 118
Ellis, H. C., 44
Engelkamp, J., 121
Ericsson, K. A., ix, xi, xii, xiii, xvi, xvii, 10, 11, 20, 55, 111

F

Fahey, J. L., xiv
Farr, M. J., x
Feltovich, P. J., ix
Field, W. H., 105
Fletcher, C. R., 53, 84
Francis, W. N., 106
Franklin, M., 2
Frankovich, L., 104
Frase, L. T., 46
Frederiksen, C. H., ix
Friesen, W. V., xiv, 118
Funke, L., xvi
Futterman, A. D., xiv

G

Geiselman, R. E., 96
Gentner, D., x
Gentner, D. R., x
Gidlund, Å., 19
Gitomer, D. H., x
Glaser, R., ix, x, 33, 48, 68
Glenberg, A. M., 110
Glenn, S. L., 63
Goodman, E., 3, 4

Goodson, J. L., 21
Gordon, P., 78, 84
Graesser, A. C., 35, 68, 75, 84, 96, 110, 119
Graves, B., ix
Greene, T. T., x, 119
Grice, H. P., 68
Griffin, M., 19
Grote, D., 63, 87
Gruneberg, M. M., 78, 85

H

Hagen, U., 5, 63, 87
Hager, J. C., 118
Harris, G., x, 69
Hasher, L., 19
Hayes, J. R., ix
Hecht, B., 69
Hemingway, E., 35
Herrmann, D., 78, 82, 86
Hertel, P. T., 44
Higbee, K. L., 78
Hinsley, D. A., ix
Hirtle, S. C., ix
Hjelmquist, E., 19
Hoffman, R. R., 119
Holgate, B., 104
Hunt, R. R., 46, 104

I

Intons-Peterson, M. J., 10, 45

J

Jacoby, L. L., 44, 104
Johnson, M. K., 34
Johnson, R. E., 23
Johnson-Laird, P. N., 110
Jones, R. M., 119

K

Kahneman, D., 104
Kay, D. S., 36, 53
Keenan, J. M., 19, 96
Kelso, M. T., x, 120
Kemeny, M. E., xiv
Kintsch, W., 19, 53
Kirk, J. W., 49, 63
Klein, G., 119
Kochnev, V. I., 118
Konijn, E. A., 118
Krampe, R. T., xi, xiv
Krebs, E. W., 78, 85
Kucera, H., 106

Author Index

L

Lachman, R., 105
Langston, M. D., 110
Lanning, G., 35
Larkin, J. H., 119
Lehmann, A. C., ix, xi, xii, xiii, xvi
Lemeignan, M., 118
Lesgold, A. M., ix, x, 96
Levenson, R. W., xiv, 118
Lewis, M. W., 33, 68
Lichtenstein, E. H., 48
Lindem, K., 110
Littlefield, J., 67
Liu, L., 84
Lockhart, L., 78, 85
Loisette, A., 78
Long, D. L., 96
Longwell, D., xvi, 4
Lorayne, H., 77, 78, 84, 85
Loyall, A. B., 119
Lucas, J., 77

M

Macauley, R., 35
MacWhinney, B., 19
Magliano, J. P., 67, 68
Mandler, G., 96
Mantyla, T., 44
Marsalis, W., xiv
Mason, R. A., 21
Mayhew, D., 19
Mayr, U., xi, xiv
McArthur, C., 69
McCallum, M. C., 44
McDaniel, M. A., 44, 67, 104
McGaw, C., 3
McKeithen, K. B., ix
McKoon, G., 96, 105
McLain-Allen, B., 119
McTeague, J., 1
Meisner, S., xvi, 4
Mekler, E., xii
Meyer, M., 110
Miller, G. A., 68
Milner, M., 111
Mohr, G., 121
Morrow, D. G., 21
Myers, J. L., 21, 44

N

Newman, D., 68
Nisbett, R. E., 55

Noice, H., xvii, xviii, 1, 10, 12, 13, 14, 15, 16, 17, 19, 26, 28, 29, 31, 32, 36, 39, 40, 41, 50, 52, 55, 56, 58, 61, 62, 64, 65, 68, 71, 74, 76, 81, 82, 83, 86, 87, 89, 90, 91, 94, 106, 121
Noice, T., xvii, xviii, 1, 71, 74, 81, 83, 86, 87, 89, 90, 91, 94, 99, 106
Norman, D. A., 78
Nyberg, S. E., 23

O

O'Brien, E. J., 21, 34, 44
Oliver, W. L., xvii, 10, 111
Olnek, M., xiii, xvi, 4, 5
Oppy, B. J., 96
Orthous, P., 118
Ortony, A., 120
Owens, J., 21, 48

P

Paivio, A., 69
Penner, B. C., x, 119
Persampieri, M., 67
Pichert, J. W., 21, 34
Pollack, N., xiii, xvi, 4, 5
Pollack, S., xiii
Polonsky, W., xiv
Polson, P. G., ix, 20
Post, T. A., ix, x, 119
Pressley, M., 67
Previto, R., xiii, xvi, 4, 5

R

Ratcliff, R., 96, 105
Reder, L. M., 44, 69
Rees, E., ix, x, 48
Reilly, W. S., 120
Reimann, P., 33, 68
Reitman, J. S., ix
Reuter, H. H., ix
Richards, D. L., 96
Robertson, S., 33
Rumelhart, D. E., 53
Rundus, D., 45
Ryan, M.-L., 120

S

Santibanez-H., G., 118
Saroyan, W., 100
Scardamalia, M., ix
Schmidt, C. F., 21

Schneider, W., xvi
Schwartz, B. J., ix
Searle, J. R., 68
Secco, T., 84
Seely, M. R., 96
Segal, E. M., 34
Sellen, O., 121
Shadbolt, N. R., 119
Shapiro, D., xiv
Shiffrin, R. M., xvi
Siegel, A. C., 34
Silverberg, L., xiv
Simon, H. A., ix, 11, 55, 56, 119
Simon, N., xii
Singer, M., 68, 75
Sloboda, J., ix, xiii, xiv
Smiley, S., 64
Smith, E. E., 48
Smith, S. H., 78, 85
Smyth, M. M., 10, 45
Snowman, J., 78, 85
Snyder, B. L., 67
Soloway, E., ix, 119
Solso, R. L., ix, xv
Spilich, G. J., 34, 48
Sridharan, N. S., 21
Stanislavski, C., 5, 6
Starkes, J. L., ix
Staszewski, J. J., 20
Stein, B. S., 17, 67
Sternberg, R. J., xi
Suh, S., 68
Swartz, M., 33
Symons, S., 67

T

Tan, E. S., 118
Taylor, J. A., ix, xii
Tesch-Roemer, C., xi

Thomson, D. M., 105
Trabasso, T., 48, 53, 67, 68, 75, 84, 96, 97
Tulving, E., 17, 105, 107, 109
Turner, T. J., 21, 34
Turnure, J. E., 67
Tyler, S. W., 44

V

Valentine, E., 77, 78, 84
Van den Broek, P. W., 48, 53, 68, 84, 96, 97
Van Dijk, T. A., 53
Van Lehn, K. A., 68, 119
Vinski, E., 104
Voss, J. G., ix, x, 34, 48, 119

W

Wang, Y., ix
Watkins, M. J., 45
Watkins, O. C., 105
Weisweiler, H., 118
Weyhrauch, P., x, 120
Wickes, B., xi
Wilding, J., 77, 78, 84
Willoughby, T., 67
Wilson, T. D., 55
Winzenz, D., 96
Wiseman, S., 105
Wittlinger, R. P., 121
Woloshyn, V. E., 67
Wood, E., 67

Z

Zechmeister, E. B., 23
Zigler, S., xiii, xvi, 4, 5
Zimmer, H. D., 121
Zwaan, R. A., 110

Subject Index

A

Acting
  essence of, xvi
  exercises for, xii
  history of instruction in, 1–5
  practice and its relationship to, xii
  textbooks on, 2–8
Actors, *see* Professional actors
Affect states, 115–116

B

Beat divisions
  recall based on differences between actors and novices, 88–91, 93–95, 97
Beats
  benefits of, 87–98
  criteria for dividing a script into, 63
  defined, 15
  dividing a scene into, 57, 91–92, 97
  goal-directed, 89
  size of, 88–89
  titles of, 92–93
Blocking
  line learning in relation to, 8, 12, 14–15, 122

C

Causality
  and comprehension, 84, 96–97
  constructing causal chains, 96–97
  as a contributor to verbatim recall, 103
  specifying causal relation between line and underlying motivation, 32–33, 96
Comprehension
  role of "why" questions to, 67–68
Confidence ratings, 107, 109

E

Elaborations
  explanatory vs. nonexplanatory, 24–25
  and memorability, 44, 67
  and mental effort, 44–45
  and its relationship to verbatim recall, 17–18
  as retrieval cues, 33–34, 44
  and rote learning, 45
  and task complexity, 44
Emotions
  emotional reality, 14
  facial expressions and experience of, 118
  illusion of, x
  and interactive drama, 119–120
  and mental states, 57–65
  recognition of, x
  universality of facial expressions, 117–118
Encoding specificity, 110
Expertise
  and the arts, ix

151

and benefit of experience, xii–xiii
and concert pianists, xv
and dancers, xv
and deliberate practice, xi
differences between novices and experts, ix, xvi–xvii
essence of, xvi
and innate talent, xi
Louis Armstrong and, xiii–xiv
musical, xiii–xiv, xv
and the 10-year rule, xiii
Experts
  modeling mental processes of, 119
Explanations
  actors' use of, 32, 67–68
  self-explanations, 68
Explanatory units
  defined, 71
  types of, 71–73

G

Goal-directed activity
  presence of, 89–91, 95
Goals, see also Intentions and Objectives
  subgoals, 161
Imagery
  actors' use of, 77–78
  mnemonists' use of, 77–86
Images
  types of, 79–80
Intentions, see also Objectives
  actors use of, 82
  deriving of, 57
  inferring of, 67
  Interactions, 25–28, 50–51, 71–74, 82
  and silent speech, 25, 27, 33
Interactive drama
  The Oz Project, x, 119–120
Internal characteristics, see also Performance characteristics
  specification of, 60–62

M

Meaning
  extracting deep, 11, 67–68, 84, 109–110, 117
Measures of accuracy
  acceptable verbatim, 93–94
  almost verbatim, 37–39, 41–42, 101–102
  deviation verbatim, 37–39
  guessing, 38, 43
  nearly verbatim, 41–42, 102
  paraphrases, 38, 42
  verbatim, 36–41, 93

Memorability
  and distinctiveness, 44
  and extracting causal relations, 32–33, 104
  and goal statements, 48, 99
  and in-depth processing, 69
  and individual-item processing, 46
  and mental effort, 44, 103–104
  and relational processing, 46
  and task complexity, 44–45
Memorization
  advice to actors on, 1–9
  factors involved in, 12
  Lorayne's approach to, 77–85
  personal advice by acting teachers on, 8–9
  T. D.'s approach to, 55–57
Memory codes, 69
Memory stores
  episodic and semantic, 105, 110–111
  retention of information in long-term, 120–121
Mental and emotional state, 57–65
Mental representation
  accessibility of, xvi–xvii, 10, 110
  actors' and novices differences in, 48
  differences in novices' and experts, ix
  redundancy in, 69
  richness of, 20–21
  structure of, 36, 53
Metastatements, 56–57, 70, 72–74, 79–80
Mnemonist
  differences between actors and a, 77–78
  Lorayne, 77–85
  memory abilities of, 77
  script learning strategies of a, 79–82
  T. E., 84
  use of peg words by, 78
Model of acting cognition, 114–117
Motivation, 33–34, 60–61, 62–63

O

Objectives, 14, 16–17, 85–86, see also Intentions
Organizing statements, 53–54, 56–57, 63

P

Performance accuracy, 108–109
Performance characteristics, see also Internal characteristics
  vs. internal characteristics, 60
  specification of, 60–63
Perspective
  adopting perspective of assigned character, 28–30, 90–91, 97
  and comprehension, 34–35

Subject Index

elaborations consistent with, 34
and memorability, 34–35
and reading time, 34
Plan recognition, *see also* Role learning
actors' use of, 16–17, 33, 63, 83, 96–97, 122
Playscripts
annotated, 99
comparing actors and mnemonist's approach to learning of, 83–85
difference between playscripts and prose, 23
dividing into idea units, 23
effect of enactment on recall of, 121–122
nature of, 33–34
one actor's attention to form and content in, 59–61, 63
and perspective, 34–35
and relational and individual-item processing, 46, 103, 104
relationship between spoken discourse and, 68–69
and verbatim recall, 40–44, 95
Problem solving
actors' learning approach and, 11, 13, 57, 99
in knowledge-rich domains, x, 57
Problem-solving units
scoring of, 58–62
Professional actors
and accuracy with which they perform playscripts, 111–113
employment and, xi–xii
learning strategy of, 11–15, *see also* Role learning
metacognition of, 66
skill acquisition and, xii–xiii
training novices in the strategies of, 99–105
use of mnemonics by, 77

R

Recall, *see also* Verbatim recall
cued recall task, 36–37
elaborated recall task, 21–35
enactment and, 121–122
following dividing a text into beats, 93–95
surprise recall task, 36, 87
temporal order, 95
of unusual Shakespearean words, 106–111
Recognition failure of recallable words, 105–111
well-learned material and, 109–110
Reliability of scoring
of cued recall protocols, 39–40
of elaborated recall task, 25–26
of recall protocols, 101
of summaries, 50
Repetition
and transfer to long-term memory, 45

Retention, *see also* Recall
beat division and its effect on, 93–95, 99–103
deep processing and, 110
long-term, 120–121
and relational and individual-item processing, 46
Retrieval
accessibility of specific lines, 7, 111
context and, 110
existing schema and ease of, 34
Role learning, *see also* Memorization
and actively using the words to obtain the goals, 114–115
aspects of text attended to during, 55–57, 69–70
and attention to exact words, 104
and automatic and controlled processing, xvi–xvii
and distributed practice, 6
and explaining the text, 46, *see also* Explanations
instructors' advice on, 8–9
organizing text during, 95–96
and overlearning, 3, 122
by recognizing the character's overall plan, 16, 33, 53, 63, 83, 96–97, 114–115
Rote learning
actors' self reports concerning, 12–13, 66
defined, 23
and forgetting, 41
and Mamet, 4–5
and meaningful material, 23
and Meisner, xvi, 4
and mental representation, 36
and recall, 13, 30–31, 40–43

S

Skilled memory theory, 20–21
Speech production
automatic and executive productions, xvii, 122
Spoken discourse, 68
Stanislavski system, 5–6, 118
Story mnemonic, 84
Summary statements
classified as emotional interactions, 48, 50
differences between actors and novices as revealed by their, 48, 51
evidence of perspective-taking in, 51–52
evidence of plan recognition in, 53
scoring of, 49–50

T

Theories of expertise
    criticisms of, x, xi
    Ericsson's model of, xi
    Glaser's model of, ix, x

V

Verbal protocols
    highlights from, 10–16
    retrospective or on-line protocols, 11, 22, 55–56, 66–68, 71
    think-aloud, 55, 66–68, 73
Verbatim recall, *see also* Recall
    and delayed testing, 19, 36, 40–43
    as a result of supplied goal statements, 99–100
    and spoken discourse, 19
Visualization, *see also* Imagery
    and deep processing, 101, 104
    and its effect on retention, 103–104
    of the other character in a scene, 101